"*Lieutenant Colonel Lock has written a fascinating and informative work on the most elite of the Army's troops and tells us what it takes to earn the coveted Black and Gold Ranger Tab. A good read for any student of the warrior ethic.*"

—Colin Powell,
General, U.S. Army (Ret.)
U.S. Secretary of State

"*JD Lock captures within* The Coveted Black and Gold *the essence of the best course in the world to prepare a man to fight and win in sustained close combat. No other course I know of, including the SEAL's premier BUDS program, prepares a man psychologically for the rigors of infantry combat. I know that I personally must have faced greater gut checks in training and combat, but nothing seems to match the seemingly endless challenges faced by my Ranger buddies and me during January patrols in the mountains of north Georgia or in the freezing waters during February in the Florida swamps. I thank God I had this Ranger School benchmark early because it served me well during the following 34 years and even into retirement. Everything seems to pale in comparison to those stark, uncompromising Ranger School tasks we had to accomplish despite the difficulties. The mission always came first and could never be compromised. Rangers, do in fact, Lead the Way!*"

—**General Wayne A. Downing,**
USA (Ret.) Third Colonel of the Regiment and former CINC,
U.S. Special Operations Command

# THE COVETED BLACK AND GOLD

A Daily Journey through

the U.S. Army Ranger

School Experience

JD Lock

*The Coveted Black and Gold: A Daily Journey Through the U.S. Army Ranger School Experience*

Second Edition (2005)

Copyright © 1993, 2001, 2005 by John Lock. All rights reserved.

No part of this book may be reproduced or retransmitted in any form or by any means without the written permission of the publisher.

This edition (2005) published by Fenestra Books™
610 East Delano Street, Suite 104, Tucson, Arizona 85705, U.S.A.
www.fenestrabooks.com

ISBN: 1-58736-368-2 (hardcover)
ISBN: 1-58736-367-4 (paperback)
Library of Congress Control Number: 2004110853

Cover photograph provided courtesy of the Ranger Training Brigade

**Do you have what it takes to earn**
*the* **Coveted Black and Gold?!**

Captain Hagan
Ranger Senior Tactical Officer,
3 June 1980

•

# DEDICATION

"I must study politics and war that my sons may have liberty to study mathematics and philosophy."
—President John Adams

To my beautiful bride and high school sweetheart, Judy, and our three lovely daughters, Jennifer, Cheryl, and Stephanie. They are the reasons I serve in the proudest profession of all, the Profession of Arms.

And to Andrew J. McGirr, my father-in-law, to whom I owe an immense debt of gratitude for having such an incredible woman for a daughter and for suggesting to me years ago that I should try to gain entrance to the United States Military Academy. It was that suggestion which ultimately led to West Point and the Coveted Black and Gold.

# CONTENTS

# FOREWORD

John Lock's *The Coveted Black and Gold: A Daily Journey Through The U.S. Army Ranger School Experience* will cause every Ranger graduate to say, "Yes, I remember that! That's the way it was!" As he reminisces, he'll also exclaim to himself, "I'm glad I did it but I'll never do it again!" Lock's attention-riveting account is based on the contraband daily log that he kept without being detected by the ever present RI (Ranger Instructor). That Lock succeeded is a tribute to his perseverance and adroitness in avoiding detection. He has achieved in writing what may be acclaimed as the seminal work on the Ranger Training Program at the Infantry School. By so doing, he has explained clearly that a Ranger is a soldier with a special attitude—self-assured, determined, demanding of himself and of those with whom he soldiers, a person for whom only the best is acceptable, a person who strives to be all that he can be.

Lock's vivid description of the Ranger Course explains why it is the most physically, mentally, and psychologically demanding training provided in the U.S. Army. The purpose of this extremely grueling regimen is to develop combat skills of carefully selected and prepared officers and enlisted men. They are required to perform effectively as small unit leaders in a realistic tactical environment under the physical and mental stress approaching that of ground combat. They develop individual combat skills and abilities through the application of leadership principles. Tactical exercises also increase the Ranger trainee's capability to plan and conduct dismounted infantry, airborne, airmobile, and amphibious independent squad and platoon-size operations. Graduates return to their units with the never-ending mission of sharing their knowledge and skills to build a better, more combat-ready Army. Receiving the Tab is only the beginning; a Ranger is expected to earn that Tab every day of his life.

While a Cadet at West Point, John Lock entered the Ranger Course in the summer of 1980 with 160 other aspirants for the coveted "Ranger Black and Gold." At graduation, 59 days later, there were only 102 standing tall, waiting to receive their Tab. Of those 102, only 72 (45 percent) were part of the original class. For the graduates, the previous fifty-nine days had been pure, unmitigated hell. The RIs were never satisfied; they always demanded a higher level of performance. They never missed the opportunity afforded by a trainee's mistake to inject a valuable lesson. They "rewarded" each lapse in security, tactics, planning or implementation with an enemy ambush or attack at unexpected times and places. These never-ending surprises stressed that, in combat, mistakes cost lives. Extreme heat, fatigue, sleep and food deprivation, insects, leeches, snakes, "wait-a-minute" vines, and what seemed like unceasing rain added to the trainee's misery and were lessons in themselves. Lock's daily recitation of these vicissitudes are fascinating and will be interesting to anyone who enjoys reading about a challenge and man's ability to overcome what may seem insurmountable. Each day's account begins with an appropriate quote from military history; these add immeasurably to the interest.

Through this purgatory, Ranger trainee John Lock maintains his perspective and asks the reader to "overlook my warped personality and perverted sense of humor." He makes jokes about the most depressing circumstances as a hedge against dropping into a deep trough of self-defeating low morale. Despite his bizarre, self-deprecating sense of humor, he is constantly aware of the potentially deadly consequences of mistakes in combat. He criticizes himself harshly for the mistakes that he makes without becoming depressed. His mental toughness keeps him going and, as it is for every trainee, is the primary determinant of whether he graduates.

Lock brings to the reader's attention the stark reality of the demands of Ranger training by indicating each day in his log the number of hours of sleep (the average is three each day) and the meals missed. Even recounting the meals missed does not indicate accurately the caloric deficiency because the "meal" received may have been only a modicum of food. But to a Ranger, any meal is a banquet!

As Lock expresses so well in "Final Thoughts," Ranger training provides a unique opportunity for a person to learn about himself. "The deprivations, adversity, exhaustion, and stress will quickly strip away any facade and reveal the true core of any man. In the process, it will assist your transformation into a warrior and leader of combat soldiers. It is an experience and accomplishment that no one can take from you."

Ranger training is the most valuable preparatory training for combat that our Army provides. It is not only the best for the leader who has completed the course but also for the soldiers he leads. Ranger graduates set the standard for our Army. By continuing such tough, realistic training, Rangers will continue to "lead the way!" They provide the hard core who set and maintain standards in training and who lead those soldiers in what is terrifying, brutal, deadly ground combat.

**Colonel Ralph Puckett, Jr. USA (Ret.)**
**Honorary Colonel of the 75th Ranger Regiment**

# THE COVETED BLACK AND GOLD

The U.S. Army Ranger School is a nine-week challenge to a man's self-confidence, physical fitness, and above all, his determination to prevail. It is a nine-week trip from hell, designed to cull out the mentally and physically weak and to make the survivors far more capable leaders. A nine week witches brew of misery; rain, mud, slime, snakes, chiggers, heat, cold, humidity, numbing fatigue, life or death situations, very little sleep or food, 70 pound rucksacks and Ranger Instructors in omnipresent wolf packs yapping, snapping and hounding the students day and night to drive out the weak.

This book takes the reader vicariously through Ranger School. I have never been to Ranger School but I have always respected greatly the accomplishment of those who have. Lieutenant Colonel (then U.S.M.A. Cadet) John Lock's diary gave me a comprehensive appreciation of what a Ranger graduate has accomplished. He spares none of the details. Carrying a hidden diary, he avoided being caught by the instructors as he scrawled daily entries. Remarkably objective, he captured it all; the hours of sleep each day (the average was 3); the meals missed; the rare humorous events; the sadness of seeing companions fail because of their own shortcomings or the inaction or incompetence of others in a patrol they were leading; the personal heroism of men in actual life-threatening situations. So far as I know, Lock's diary is the only day-to-day student chronology of the great stress and pressure on an aspiring Ranger to perform 100 percent correctly while being physically miserable, worn out and severely undernourished.

I highly recommend this book to those who would like to know more about Army Rangers. And to those who are about to go into Ranger School, it will provide an excellent "recon."

**Lieutenant General Harold G. Moore, USA (Ret.)**
**Co-author of the New York Times Best Seller *We Were Soldiers Once…and Young***

A must read to understand the Ranger community and for those aspiring to become RANGER QUALIFIED—the right of passage for leaders who can be depended on when the going gets tough. The coveted BLACK and GOLD establishes a standard for setting the example, leading the way and to live by for the rest of your life.

**Brigadier General Dave Grange, USA (Ret.)**
**7th Colonel of the Regiment**

Professional soldier and West Point graduate John Lock takes you into the heart of America's most intense military experience, United States Army Ranger School. Here is Ranger training up close and personal, so real that you feel the pain, taste the sweat, and learn just what it takes to wear The Coveted Black and Gold.

**Colonel Daniel P. Bolger**
**Author of *Savage Peace***

In prose as spare and sharp as a soldier's bayonet, John Lock shows what young men of character can and will endure in pursuit of a dream to become the best.

**Ed Ruggero**
**USMA graduate and author of *38 North Yankee***

The author is a wonderful writer who has captured the Ranger course experience like no other I have read. If published in its present form, it would likely do well as preparatory reading for those who are about to go to Ranger school and for those who are its graduates, an insightful narrative describing the challenges they faced.

**Manuscript Review Comments AUSA, 20 July 2000**

# INTRODUCTION

> After the train had been captured by 150 Boers, the last four men, though completely surrounded, and with no cover, continued to fire until three were killed, the fourth wounded. On the Boers asking the survivor the reason why they had not surrendered, he replied, "Why, man, we are the Gordon Highlanders."
>
> Lord Kitchener,
> Telegram from Pretoria, to Edward VII
> (10 August 1901)

For more than two hundred years, U.S. Army Rangers have earned their unrivaled reputation as the world's premier warriors with bravery, blood, and sacrifice. They are among the most elite, if not *the* most elite, combat soldiers in the world. Being a Ranger is a function of attitude and a state of mind, as well as a matter of skills and training, and it is the mission of the US Army Ranger School to bring all of these attributes together.

To begin with, one has to be an excellent soldier to attend this course. Just being physically tough does not do it. One must be mentally tough, also. The physical demands, unrelenting pressure, psychological stress, minimal food and rest will either break the Ranger student and make him quit or forge a significantly more confident and capable combat leader.

The Ranger School course of instruction is a handshake with reality, a rite of passage. It is a fraternity initiation...an initiation into a highly select band of warriors within the profession of arms that only a select few will attempt to join...with even fewer meeting the standard for inclusion. It will build and mold soldiers...tough, resolute soldiers who will be hard physically and even harder psychologically. It will never graduate a large percentage of those who attempt the challenge, for the course is too long and too hard for all but the most tenacious and resolute.

On average, only 3,000 soldiers a year are offered the opportunity to earn the Coveted Black and Gold Ranger Tab...as the Ranger Instructors are prone to refer to the qualification. Of those Ranger candidates who begin the grueling nine-week course each year and who are presumably ready for the challenge, less than half graduate. Of the half who graduate, half of them will have repeated one of the course's three phases. Statistically speaking, in the end, only 25 percent of those handpicked to attend actually complete the course on the first try.

*The Coveted Black and Gold* chronicles the Ranger School experience of a United States Military Academy cadet during Ranger Class 10-80. In June of 1980, a total of sixty-one cadets from West Point Class of 1982 entered this Ranger class. On 31 July, only thirty-nine of those sixty-one Ranger candidates graduated—a passing rate of 64 percent.

Little has been written about the course itself, much less the actual day-to-day experiences of a Ranger student. From that perspective, alone, *The Coveted Black and Gold* is exceptionally unique, for it is the only book or record of the daily struggle and challenge of one of the world's toughest military training schools.

In that I have captured the experience chronologically, to include hours slept and meals consumed each day, I have elected to maintain my notes as a daily journal rather than convert it to a more traditional novel format. For the most part, journals are written in narrative, story form. But most of these journals cover non-replicable events, such as war. Ranger School, on the other hand, is a replicable event. For fourteen classes a year, the same events occur on the same days, relatively speaking.

To those who have experienced the course and to those who aspire to it, the reason for this chronological approach will become quite clear as you read of the experience. Ranger School is a journey that must be taken one day at a time. Though the timing for some of the events may have changed over the past number of years, the experiences themselves have not. It is the cumulative effect of each of those days, the arduous work, the deprivation, the misery, that lead to what is ultimately called the Ranger School experience. Ranger School is a structured series of events that earns one the right and privilege to be awarded the Ranger Tab, to be worn with pride on the left shoulder of a soldier's uniform. To remove the structure, to remove the sequence of those events, to remove the daily entry of meals eaten and hours slept would seriously diminish and distort the view of that experience.

There are two reasons why this first-hand account exists. The first reason was merely a matter of survival. I made entries each day in an attempt to remain awake during low levels of intensity...usually while sitting in a patrol base. The second reason was to chronicle an exclusive, and what I thought would be a once in a lifetime, experience. While I was not always successful at the first...as my journal will attest, I was on target with the second. No part of this work is contrived or fiction. I have attempted to remain true to the original entries hoping that the actual words written at the time will convey some sense of the experience. The only literary license I have taken is to expand in some areas of the journal to explain events in further or clearer detail.

To those seeking to understand what Ranger School and being a Ranger are all about, I hope this work will assist you to some degree. Beware, though, of the following two caveats. While certain leadership techniques work for some people, the same techniques may not work for others. As you read this memoir, you will note that there are some rather unorthodox...for the lack of a better term...methods that worked for me. They may not necessarily work for anyone else, and they may not have been the best techniques for me to use at the time. One key to being a successful leader is the ability to identify those techniques that will work for you. Do not attempt to be someone you are not. Take the best you see in others and make it a part of your leadership philosophy. If it isn't your style, don't force it.

The second caveat is to forewarn you that there is no 'cookie-cutter solution' to Ranger school. This memoir is nothing more than that—a memoir. One Ranger's experience that is the same or similar to thousands of others. The only difference between anyone else's experience and mine is the fact that I recorded them. There are no secrets to reveal. This journal describes what Ranger School is like. To travel this road as I did does not guarantee success, for this journey is based much more on who you are than on what you know.

For those who are graduates and who already proudly wear the Coveted Black and Gold, these entries may help clear the haze that has hindered your ability to recall many of your own Ranger School experiences, thus bringing to mind a number of forgotten stories and anecdotes. For many of you, you will only need to change the names and the dates to read your own similar story. For those who desire to attend and earn the Coveted Black and Gold, I hope this chronicle vicariously provides you with a view of what it will take to earn that precious strip of colored cloth.

There are three people whom I would like to acknowledge specifically.

The first person is Mr. James Thorpe who was owner and editor of The Shoe String Press. Mr. Thorpe passed away in 1994. I am saddened by his loss both personally and professionally, for he was the only publisher to respond with a constructive criticism of my work when I initially attempted to have it published in 1993—two and a half pages of constructive criticism to be exact. Many of his remarks were insightful, on the mark, and incorporated in my many subsequent revisions. I owe him a debt of gratitude.

The second person I'd like to thank is Colonel Ralph Puckett, an exceptionally enthusiastic supporter of my works and the quintessential Ranger. Former company commander of the 8th Ranger Company during the Korean Conflict, a two-time holder of the Distinguished Service Cross, member of the Ranger Hall of Fame, Ranger Puckett is still the ultimate warrior, setting the standard for the members of the Regiment and bedding down with them in the field with nothing more than a poncho liner and an over-abundance of "Hoo Ahh." Thank you, sir, for your friendship and for the sterling example you set for all of us to strive to emulate.

I also need to acknowledge the assistance of Lieutenant Colonel Lester W. Knotts, friend, USMA classmate, Ranger Buddy, and fellow member of the profession of arms. Les' assistance in helping me to transcribe my journal stylistically, grammatically, and factually was invaluable. Unfortunately, I still cannot forgive him for his patrol on Day 36. Sorry, buddy.

U.S. Army Rangers are highly trained and motivated professionals who live by a code called "The Ranger Creed." It is sacrosanct. It is a way of life, a guide for how Rangers conduct themselves. It is the source that binds through loyalty the individual to his Ranger Buddies and to his unit.

## THE RANGER CREED

Recognizing that I volunteered as a Ranger, fully knowing the hazards of my chosen profession, I will always endeavor to uphold the prestige, honor, and high esprit de corps of the Rangers.

Acknowledging the fact that a Ranger is a more elite soldier who arrives at the cutting edge of battle by land, sea, or air, I accept the fact that as a Ranger my country expects me to move farther, faster, and fight harder than any other soldier.

Never shall I fail my comrades. I will always keep myself mentally alert, physically strong, and morally straight, and I will shoulder more than my share of the task, whatever it may be. One hundred percent and then some.

Gallantly will I show the world that I am a specially selected and well-trained soldier. My courtesy to superior officers, my neatness of dress, and care of equipment shall set the example for others to follow.

Energetically will I meet the enemies of my country. I shall defeat them on the field of battle for I am better trained and will fight with all my might. Surrender is not a Ranger word. I will never leave a fallen comrade to fall into the hands of the enemy, and under no circumstances will I ever embarrass my country.

Readily will I display the intestinal fortitude required to fight on to the Ranger objective and complete the mission, though I be the lone survivor. Rangers Lead the Way!

Command Sergeant Major Neil R. Gentry, 1974

# CHAPTER 1

# THE RANGER TRAINING BRIGADE

**May a dying soldier's last words on the field of battle never be "If I'd only been better trained."**

Anonymous

**PURPOSE:** To teach and develop Combat Arms Functional Skills relevant to fighting the close combat, direct fire battle. Leadership development is a tertiary benefit to the student—NOT THE COURSE PURPOSE. Selected officer and enlisted personnel will be challenged by requiring them to perform effectively as small unit leaders in a realistic tactical environment under mental and physical stress approaching that found in combat. It provides the student with practical experience in the application of the tactics and techniques of Ranger operations in wooded, lowland swamp and mountainous environments. Emphasis is placed on development of fundamental individual skills through the application of the principles of leadership while further developing military skills in the planning and conduct of dismounted infantry, airborne, air assault and amphibious squad and platoon size combat operations.

Ranger Course Pamphlet

The Ranger Department of the Infantry School, located at Fort Benning, Georgia, was initially established in 1951 with the first class commencing training in January 1952 and graduating two months later in March. Over time, the Ranger school came to be staffed with a cadre of 300 carefully selected men. Prior to Vietnam, the 923 hours of training focused on patrolling as a tool for teaching basic infantry tactics and small-unit leadership skills up to platoon level.

Based on Vietnam experiences, the entire curriculum was revised in mid-1965 to address wartime requirements. Expanded to 1,149 hours, the course became a performance-based field training experience to instill the skills, physical stamina, and mental toughness and conditioning necessary to lead long range patrols into enemy territory for extended lengths of time. The first class to undergo this new plan of instruction was the Ranger class of 8 July to 7 September 1965.

During 1966, the army staff took a very hard look at making Ranger training mandatory for all newly commissioned army officers. That year, a panel chaired by General Ralph E. Haines, Jr., recommended that such a concept be implemented. On 16 August 1966, the Chief of Staff of the Army, General Harold K. Johnson, directed it so. Looking to eventually triple class output from an average of 1,000 per year to over 3,000, Johnson doubled the classes of early 1967 and sliced a week from the first phase at Fort Benning. As a result, the annual Ranger program went from ten 130-man classes to fourteen 220-man classes. Starting in June 1967, it became mandatory for every newly commissioned Regular Army (RA) officer to attend the course.

The cherished hallmark of Ranger volunteerism had been eliminated. Disgruntled RA officers minimized their efforts while they attended the course while others intentionally failed the Ranger entrance requirements or deliberately failed other aspects of the course. The school began to be pressured to ease the course standards to increase graduation statistics.

On 28 January 1970, General Westmoreland directed The Infantry School (TIS) to thoroughly reevaluate the Ranger school course. Among the recommendations in regards to the curriculum, TIS authorized the awarding of the Ranger Tab to all course graduates, to include the bottom-level graduates who, until then, had not been awarded the Tab. Until that time, those 'at the bottom' had been designated "Completed"...which meant they had successfully finished the course of instruction but had not met the standards necessary for award of the Tab.

Despite some general officer in-fighting in late 1970 and early 1971, Westmoreland finally directed on 21 June 1971, that Ranger training for all RA officers would no longer be compulsory and reverted to being voluntary, once again.

While the department has undergone a number of transformations to arrive at where it is today, the experiences of 1952 Ranger School graduates are not dissimilar to those of the most recent Ranger School graduate. In August 1987, the Ranger Department became its own independent entity when it was separated from The Infantry School and reestablished as the Ranger Training Brigade. What had originally been designated as Ranger companies were redesignated as Ranger Training Battalions.

Prior to 1983 and the institution of the Desert Phase, the overall length of the course was fifty-nine days. With the addition of the Desert Phase, the course expanded to sixty-five days with the sequence of training running Fort Benning Phase, Mountain Phase, Florida Phase, and Desert Phase (Dugway Proving Grounds, Utah). In October of 1991, the course was increased to sixty-eight days and the sequence was changed to Fort Benning, Desert (Fort Bliss, Texas), Mountain, and Florida.

In May of 1995, the school underwent its most recent change when the Desert Phase was discontinued. Aspects of this Phase were incorporated in the remaining phases, thus shortening the duration of the overall course to sixty-one days with an average of 19.6 hours of training per day, seven days per week. The Benning and Mountain Phases are twenty-one days in length while the Florida Phase is seventeen days. The remaining two days are allocated for travel, maintenance, in/out processing, and graduation.

In this book, I provide an overview at the start of each Ranger School phase. Keep in mind that the course's schedule is flexible, as is its plan of instruction. While the actual sequence and number of days may deviate slightly from those stated, the experience will not.

As for who may attend, all male officers and NCOs from United States or Allied countries may apply for Ranger Training. Those soldiers who are the equivalent of a corporal or below must obtain a waiver from the first colonel in their chain of command. All applicants must be in top physical condition and in good health. Previous injuries such as heat injuries or hypothermia can be grounds for disqualification.

Since its establishment in 1952, Ranger school's focus has been on training the individual. The intent of the course is to train officers and NCOs who will return to their units to train their soldiers what they, themselves, have been taught. The school's goal is to graduate at least 3,000 Rangers a year but, with an attrition rate of over 65 percent, this goal is not attainable.

One of the primary reasons for such a significant attrition rate is the realistic, stressed induced, environment in which the Ranger students must prove themselves. A great deal of effort is made to simulate the stresses associated with combat. Stress is induced by reducing meals to one or two per day. On average, a Ranger School student receives 5,000 calories for a 6,000 calorie work day, conducting long training days that can run, on average from 0500 to 0200, and placing students in positions of responsibility that require them to make timely and accurate decisions. As the student progresses through the course from squad, section, and platoon sized operations, the body and mind are progressively fatigued by sleep deprivation and body mass loss. On average, a Ranger will lose 30 pounds from his reporting weight.

By graduation day, the latest recipient of the Coveted Black and Gold usually finds himself in the worst shape of his life.

Stress is essential to leadership. Living with stress, know-ing how to handle pressure, is necessary for survival. It is related to a man's ability to wrest control over his own destiny from the circumstances that surround him.

Admiral James Stockdale,
'Education for Leadership
and Survival,'
MILITARY ETHICS, 1987

# CHAPTER 2

# THE STANDARD

Training is all-encompassing and should be related to every-
thing a unit does or can have happen to it.
Lt. General Arthur S. Collins, Jr.
COMMON SENSE TRAINING, 1978

The course emphasis is on practical, realistic, and strenuous field training designed to develop combat arms functional skills relevant to fighting the close combat, direct fire battle. Training is conducted in units that vary in size from an infantry rifle squad to platoon that travel distances up to 30 kilometers per mission, primarily at night, under all types of weather conditions. Fatigue, hunger, mental and emotional stresses are replicated conditions to which the Ranger student is exposed. This provides an environment in which each man can demonstrate his ability to make quick, sound, and forceful decisions under simulated combat conditions.

As stated earlier, on average, nearly half of those who begin with a class will never earn the Tab. Of those who do earn the Coveted Black and Gold, only twenty-five percent do so with their original class. How does this 25 percent succeed? They meet the following criteria:

## BENNING PHASE:
- Pass the APFT: fifty-two pushups, sixty-two sit-ups, and a two-mile run in running shoes in less than fourteen minutes and fifty-five seconds.
- Complete six chin-ups.
- Pass the Combat Water Survival Test (CWST): fifteen-meter swim, three-meter diving board swim, blindfolded submerge and ditch.
- Ranger Stakes: successfully complete seven of ten tasks on the first or second try.
- Land navigation test: successfully pass the day and night course on the first or second try.
- Complete the five mile Ranger Run.
- Complete all but two PT runs (as a minimum).
- Complete the twelve-mile tactical road march in full combat gear
- Water confidence test: walk across a log 30 feet above the water, drop 35 feet from a rope into Victory Pond, descend down a 200 feet 'slide for life'.
- Complete the Darby Queen obstacle course.
- Receive at least one positive leadership evaluation.

## MOUNTAIN PHASE:
- Knot test: successfully pass eight of the twelve knots.
- Pass the rappelling belay test.
- Successfully perform three daytime rappels, including one with rucksack, and one using only two bounds against the cliff.
- Successfully perform a 200-foot night rappel (or 60-foot fixed rope descent in adverse weather).
- Pass a minimum of one patrol.
- Receive at least one positive leadership evaluation.

## FLORIDA PHASE:
- Pass a minimum of one patrol.
- Receive at least one positive leadership evaluation.

\*\*\*\*\*

Each task within a phase must be successfully accomplished in order to advance to the next phase.

\*\*\*\*\*

## OVERALL:

- Pass a total of fifty percent of all patrols with at least one of the passes in a primary leadership position as Patrol Leader or Patrol Sergeant.
- Pass at least two of four peer ratings—one per phase plus an end of course rating that evaluates individual leadership qualities and Ranger skills.
- Fail to accumulate the equivalent of eight major minus spot results...formally known as Critical Incident Report (CIR) Spot Reports (three minor spot reports equal a major). Note: a total of five major minus spot reports results in a review of the student's status.
- Fail to receive a negative Special Observation Report (SOR) approved by the brigade chain of command.
- Avoid accumulating more than 72 hours of missed training through all three phases.

For those students who excel, there are academic honors and awards designed to recognize outstanding achievement during the course:

**William O. Darby Award:** To the student who clearly demonstrated himself a cut above all other Rangers.

**Distinguished Honor Graduate:** To the student with the best overall performance. In the absence of anyone meeting this criteria, the top graduate may be designated Honor Graduate.

**Ralph Puckett Award:** Top officer graduate.

**Glenn M. Hall Award:** Top enlisted graduate.

**Merrill's Marauder Award:** To the officer and enlisted soldier who scored highest on land navigation.

**Benjamin Church Leadership Award:** To the officer and enlisted soldier who exemplified outstanding leadership throughout the entire course.

**Non Commissioned Officer Association Award:** To the top enlisted graduate.

As one can see, evaluations, awards, and honors are conducted both on an individual and group basis. Individually, tasks are identified and individual standards are established. For the most part, these standards are very objective in nature.

Other standards, though, are based upon group dynamics. This is where being a team player is important. Whether it's peer ratings or patrol operations, you will not be successful if you attempt to go it alone. 'Lone Rangers' usually do not succeed in Ranger School.

While failure in any of these events will result in being dropped from your class, it does not necessarily mean that you will be disenrolled from the course. Negative spot reports or SORs are normally the only failures that result in an automatic dismissal from the course with no option to return. Usually, all other failures result in a recycle to the following class.

Which event is the most difficult to train for? Most assuredly it is the patrol itself for there are so many subtasks and responsibilities. Not only must one be prepared to receive the order, but he must be prepared to plan for, issue, rehearse, and execute the mission. The leadership rotates among the students so everyone is at least evaluated once in each phase. Students in danger of failing are usually given more time as a leader in later phases to allow them to improve their performance and attempt to achieve that overall fifty percent goal.

**Individual training is the foundation on which unit effectiveness is built. It is the source of a soldier's confidence and trust in the Army.**

Lieutenant General Arthur S. Collins, Jr.
COMMON SENSE TRAINING, 1978

*****

At the start of each phase, I have included an introduction that describes the phase as it is conducted as of this writing. While one may note that there are some program differences between now and 1980—when the author attended the course—the overall experiences are still exceptionally similar.

*****

# CHAPTER 3

# OUR PRE-RANGER DAYS

**The man who spends more sleepless nights with his army and who works harder in drilling his troops runs the fewest risks in fighting the foe.**

The Emperor Maurice
THE STRATEGIKON, c.AD 600

While pre-Ranger training is not a mandatory prerequisite for attending Ranger School, no responsible unit or organization would send its soldiers to Ft. Benning without it, for, without this preparatory training, the soldier will most likely fail.

One unit that does make this type of training mandatory is the 75th Ranger Regiment. For those members selected to attend, their training—referred to as the Ranger Indoctrination Program (RIP)—commences a month prior to the start of their scheduled Ranger School class date when the Ranger candidate begins a formal training and evaluation period by regiment cadre on numerous Ranger basics: raids, reconnaissance, patrols, and ambushes. Woven throughout the course of this training is an added emphasis on land navigation and physical training. To prevent mental and physical deterioration, the candidates are not deprived of food or sleep—there will be enough of that later.

The program can be judged as extremely successful for the Ranger Regiment's attrition rate in Ranger School is less than ten percent. And for those who believe Regiment soldiers have it made, you are sadly mistaken for even more is expected, and demanded, of these soldiers than any other.

Pre-Ranger training is also offered by the 4th Ranger Training Battalion one week prior to each class reporting date. Referred to as "Zero Week," the nearly weeklong optional training event is intended to produce a "mentally hardened soldier who has acclimated to the Georgia weather and passed the APFT and CWST." For those who pass the APFT and CWST during Zero Week, it counts for Ranger School. For those who fail, they are allowed to retest on Day One of the Ranger Course. In addition, Zero Week conducts PT daily, performs the Five-Mile Run, Land Navigation, Ranger Stakes, and various other Troop Leading Procedure functions.

Zero Week is not intended to make one proficient in any one task. Nor is it designed to train Ranger School candidates to graduate the Ranger School Course. It has clearly demonstrated, however, that those who do participate in the program are less likely to be eliminated during the first five days of the course…the period of greatest attrition.

*****

That which now follows are the notes from my Ranger School journal that were safely buried—along with a small camera—under three layers of waterproofing. Each entry identifies the date and the specific day in reference to the school reporting date—Ranger Day. At the completion of each day commencing with R-Day (or Day 1), I've noted the total number of hours slept and the number of meals consumed for that particular day.

Contrary to the month-long pre-Ranger training of a Ranger Regiment candidate, we United States Military Academy (USMA) cadets underwent a less intense but no less all-encompassing experience. In reality, our training began the previous summer, prior to our selection to attend Ranger School during a period of training referred to as

Camp Buckner. It was during that six-week training period we were taught the fundamentals of patrolling and various other individual soldier skills. Following our selection to attend the course, our primary focus turned to land navigation—conditioning was of little concern for all of us were required by our curriculum to be involved in some form of athletic activity. After spending many days and a few evenings moving across the mountainous terrain of West Point, most of us became rather proficient at reading maps and finding a specific point on the ground.

Upon completion of the academic term, each of us was authorized a few days leave. The vast majority went home where we devoted the remaining time to completing our packing list of items to take to the school, in addition to attending to a few other last minute details. Wanting to ensure that we had a few days to acclimate and orient ourselves to a new climate and terrain, our USMA Ranger Liaison Officer—whom I will also refer to as our USMA Tac—had us report to Fort Benning, Georgia, four days prior to the start of the course. It is at that point my account begins.

*****

## 30 MAY 1980 (R-Day <RANGER DAY> minus 4)

Well, it's been one of those days. I jumped aboard my flight out of Philadelphia with no problem, but from there things deteriorated rapidly. On the 727, I had two women crowd into my seat by the window even though the plane was not fully loaded. They were both rather senior in age and not very inclined to talk. While one of them was coughing non-stop in one of my ears, a little tike who must have had the healthiest pair of lungs that I've ever heard was screaming in the other. These circumstances did not make for an enjoyable two-hour flight. As the day grew longer, it progressively worsened. As luck would have it, we set down in Atlanta at 1430 hours, after a long delay, just as my connecting flight to Columbus, Georgia was taking off.

Needing to report by 1800, I had to look into some other options. The carrier I was flying had all of its later flights to Columbus filled, so I had to resort to a local 'puddle jumper' organization. What an adventure. The flight was supposed to depart at 1600, which, of course, did not happen. An hour after its scheduled departure time, we finally walked out onto the tarmac to load.

At first, I thought it was a little Piper Cub. How we squeezed eighteen people into that plane I'll never know. Then, as we gained speed vibrating down the runway, I happened to glance down at the tire through my window to see a white streak continually flash by as the tire rotated. Curiosity had the best of me. What could it be? Once airborne, the wheel stopped turning and I had my answer. The tire was so worn, its inner white lining was showing through.

Somehow, we—some fellow cadets I had linked up with in Atlanta and I—made it to Columbus. Unfortunately, the same could not be said about our luggage, for it didn't arrive until two flights later. But what the hell. This is probably nothing more than an omen of how Ranger School will be.

We arrived at Fort Benning around 1900 and settled into our Bachelor Officer's Quarters (BOQ) rooms. Our USMA Tac is on hand. He will serve as a liaison as we go through the course. In addition, he has planned for us a couple of days worth of training prior to the start of the course to expose us to the local terrain and to begin our acclimation process. The weather here is certainly a bit more warm and humid than that farther north at West Point.

## 31 MAY 1980 (PreRanger: R-Day minus 3)

Well, it's started. One of our more aggressively motivated classmates came around banging on our doors at 0555 hours.

From 0900 to 1600 land navigation. The weather was excellent: high humidity, temp 90-95 degrees. I think every spider in the United States wove a web between the trees on this land nav course—especially the big, black and yellow ones with the thick silk that clings to you. We ran two courses. I failed the first course; basically a result of being somewhat lethargic. Perked up and remained focused on the second course and easily maxed that one.

Our USMA Ranger Liaison Officer is working hard to train and motivate our group. I've never seen a more gung-ho individual in my entire life. Hopefully, all of his "Rangers Lead the Way!" will lead to a high success rate approximately 62 days from now, though I do believe it will take just a wee bit more than that to earn the Tab.

Got our Ranger haircuts this evening—one style fits all—and I must admit we look pretty nasty. Most of us have some degree of tan. Consequently, the absence of hair leaves us with what appears to be white skull caps—or black skull caps as the case may be. Our appearance probably serves as a great form of birth control for no self-respecting woman would be inclined to be associated with any of us. Some of the heads are great works of art. Les', in particular, looks like a contoured relief map. Maybe we can use it as a training aid during the planning phase of our patrols.

Feet hurt a little from my new jungle boots. I'm beginning to believe I made a significant mistake not breaking them in earlier. Ended the day pulling ticks off my body—seven to be exact.

## 1 JUNE 1980 (PreRanger: R-Day minus 2)

One more day to go. Have to admit this waiting around is very trying. Today was much the same as yesterday. Two land nav courses. Maxed out on both. The second course took only an hour and fifteen minutes of the allotted three and a half hours. The undergrowth wasn't quite as bad and it was a different course. Few 'wait-a-minute' vines; the kind that hang from trees and appear to burrow into the ground. They are sticky tentacles of prickly delay that are exceptionally tough, if not impossible, to move through. The snakes are still about, as are the ant 'high rise' apartments. They are amazing. Some of these mounds of Georgia red clay are four to five feet tall!

Took advantage of the opportunity to contact the outside world. That luxury will not be available to us much longer. Ended up calling home and Donnie, my USMA roommate.

## 2 JUNE 1980 (PreRanger: R-Day minus 1)

The final day of train-up. Caught up on last minute purchases—about $41 worth. Ugh. With our limited income it feels like $401. Fifteen dollars alone for five OD green T-shirts.

As for our USMA liaison officer, he is working very hard on our behalf. He wants to see everyone get the Tab and is doing his best to get us prepared. Speaking of the Tab, some cadets are carrying a Ranger Tab with them as a motivational force; not a bad idea, probably—unless, of course, you get caught by a Ranger Instructor (RI) with one in your possession.

Sampled the Officer's Club—a last meal for the condemned? The Infantry Bar, I-Bar, was pretty good. Had a few brews and the Go-Go dancer was very entertaining.

# CHAPTER 4

# RANGER SCHOOL: BENNING PHASE

Perhaps somewhere in primal reaches of our Army's memory, left over from the days ten thousand years ago when armies first began, there's a simple and fundamental formula:

SKILL + WILL = KILL

Colonel Dandridge M. Malone
ARMY MAGAZINE, September 1979

Phase I of Ranger School is currently twenty-one days in duration and conducted by the 4th Ranger Training Battalion in the heavily forested terrain of Fort Benning, Georgia. Reporting to the Ranger Training Brigade with military and medical records in hand and no rank or service insignia on his uniform, each candidate undergoes an in-processing procedure that begins with, as all things military must, paperwork. Upon completion of the administrative paperwork, the Army Physical Fitness Test—APFT—is administered. The school minimums are fifty-two pushups, sixty-two sit-ups, and a two-mile run in running shoes in less than fourteen minutes and fifty-five seconds.

Upon completion of the run, each student must complete six chin-ups. With few exceptions, Ranger students are provided the opportunity to retest any physical or training event they initially fail.

The three-event Combat Water Survival Test is the next challenge to be faced by the prospective Ranger candidate. The uniform for each of these events is fatigues, boots, webbed gear with canteens and ammo pouches, and rifle. The first event is a fifteen-meter swim. The second event has the student submerge, remain underwater while discarding weapon and equipment, and then swim to the side of the pool. The final event requires the student, while blindfolded, to walk off the end of a three-meter diving board, remove the blindfold, and swim to the side of the pool. During the course of each of these events, the student must show no undo fear or panic and, with the exception of the second event, must not lose any of his equipment. For those who have trained properly at home station, the APFT and swim test will prove to be the easiest events to pass at Ranger School.

At this point, the student is assigned to one of three companies, Alpha, Bravo, or Charlie. The remainder of the day is spent being issued equipment, completing additional paperwork, and being assigned a Ranger Buddy. Rangers always do things as part of a team and the Ranger Buddy concept dates back to the Second World War and Darby's Rangers. Ranger Buddies often remain friends for life.

The APFT begins a segment of training at Camp Rogers referred to as the Ranger Assessment Phase (RAP). RAP was implemented with the first class of 1992 and is a significant change of instruction from prior classes that immediately began the arduous 24-hour per day training. Testing and evaluation is still conducted but in a much less threatening or hostile environment during this period. Students are assessed on previous Ranger School favorites such as the predawn eight minutes per mile runs—be forewarned, the eight minute pace is the Army minimum or standard that the RIs will improve on, the five-mile Ranger run (No Retest), a 12-mile tactical road march (No Retest), as well as day and night land navigation courses.

In general, the RAP schedule is as follows:

**Day 1:**
> (1) Event – APFT.
> (2) Event – CWST.
> (3) Medical Considerations class.

**Day 2:**
> (1) Event – PT. Standard: 5-mile formation run in 40:00 minutes or less after PT IAW FM 21-20.
> (2) Event – Land navigation review.
> (3) Event – Terrain Association.
> (4) Event – Hand to Hand Combat.

**Day 3:**
> (1) Event – Night/Day Land Navigation Test.
> (2) Event – Rangers-In-Action Demonstration.
> (3) Event – Water Confidence Test
> (4) Event – Battle Drill/Patrolling Techniques
> (5) Event – Hand to Hand Combat

**Day 4:**
> (1) Event – 3-Mile Ranger Run/Malvesti Field Obstacle Course
> (2) Event – Ranger Stakes.
> (3) Event – Day Land Navigation Retest (Night/Day).
> (4) Event – Battle Drill/Patrolling Techniques.

**Day 5:**
> (1) Event – 12 mile Foot March
> (2) Event – Troop Leading Procedures
> (3) Event – Hand To Hand Combat

Following the APFT and CWST of Day 1, Day 2 of RAP is primarily devoted to familiarization. Day 3 finds the Ranger candidate wet, once more, as he is run through the Water Confidence Test. Conducted throughout the year and suspended only when the water temperature falls below 39°F or the air temperature or wind chill is lower than 38°F, the Ranger Student must climb a ladder, walk across a log 30 feet above the water, and drop 35 feet from a rope into Victory Pond. The student then exits the water, climbs a 60-foot tower, and suspends from a pulley as he descends down a 200-foot 'slide for life' cable back into the water.

Day 4 of RAP proves to be the busiest day of all as the candidates begin the day by tackling the Confidence Course. Consisting of a series of events, the course is designed to build agility and endurance.

1. Climb a four-meter high log fence without ropes
2. Enter and negotiate the worm pit (my favorite); a shallow, muddy 25-meter length obstacle covered by knee-high barbed wire. The obstacle must be negotiated on one's back and belly.
3. Cross a five-meter long mud pit by going hand-over-hand along rafters/rungs 10 feet above the pit.
4. Climb a cargo net and then slide down a rope on the other side.

For those who complete the course early, there are always the perennial favorites: pushups and flutter kicks. Of course, there is also the option of going through the course a second time.

Prior to his arrival at Harmony Church, each Ranger candidate must have his commander verify his proficiency in twenty specific military skills that are deemed necessary for successful completion of the Ranger Course:

1. Call for and adjust indirect fire (STP 21-24 SMCT, pg 55, 061-283-6003)
2. Camouflage yourself and your individual equipment (STP 21-1 SMCT, pg 393, 051-191-1361)
3. Use KTC 1400 (STP 7-11BCHM14-SM-TG, pg 3-457, 113-573-4006)

4. Navigate from one point on the ground to another point while dismounted (STP 21-24 SMCT, pg 21, 071-329-1006)
5. Determine the grid coordinates of a point on a military map (STP 21-1 SMCT, pg 76, 071-329-1002)
6. Determine a magnetic azimuth using a lensatic compass (STP 21-1 SMCT, pg 90, 071-329-1003)
7. Determine the elevation of a point on the ground using a map (STP 21-24 SMCT, pg 36, 071-329-1004)
8. Determine a location on the ground by terrain association (STP 21-1 SMCT, pg 87, 071-329-1005)
9. Measure distance on a map (STP 21-1 SMCT, pg 105, 071-329-1008)
10. Convert azimuths (STP 21-24 SMCT, pg 28, 071-329-1009)
11. Determine azimuth using a protractor (STP 21-24 SMCT, pg 45, 071-510-0001)
12. Orient a map using a lensatic compass (STP 21-24 SMCT, pg 30, 071-329-1011)
13. Orient a map to the ground by map-terrain association (STP 21-1 SMCT, pg 72, 071-329-1012)
14. Locate an unknown point on a map and on the ground by intersection (STP 21-24 SMCT, pg 39, 071-329-1014)
15. Locate an unknown point on a map and on the ground by resection (STP 21-24 SMCT, pg 42, 071-329-1015)
16. Prime explosives non-electrically (STP7-11BCHM14-SM-TG, pg 3-480, 051-193-1003)
17. Clear a misfire (Demolitions) (STP 7-11BCHM14-SM-TG, pg 3-488, 051-193-2030)
18. Practice preventive medicine (STP 21-1 SMCT, pg 338, 081-831-1043)
19. Prepare an M136 Launcher for firing (STP 21-1 SMCT, pg 199, 071-054-0001)
20. Operate night vision goggles AN/PVS-7 (STP 7-11BCHM-SM-TG, pg 3-340, 071-315-0030)

There are also a series of ten tests referred to as the Ranger Stakes conducted during the RAP on Day 4. These tests provide a quick means of identifying students' abilities and skills on the following specific individual tasks that deal with communications and light infantry weapons.

1. Maintain an M60 MG (STP 7-11BCHM14-SM-TG, pg 3-270, 071-312-3025)
2. Load an M60 MG (STP 21-1 SMCT, pg 251, 071-312-3027)
3. Prepare a Range Card for an M60 MG (STP 7-11BCHM14-SM-TG pg 3-260, 071-312-3007)
4. Perform operator maintenance on an M249 MG (STP 7-11BCHM14-SM-TG, pg 3-130, 071-312-4025)
5. Operate an M249 MG (STP 7-11BCHM14-SM-TG, pg 3-151, 071-312-4027)
6. Employ an M18A1 Claymore mine (STP 21-1 SMCT, pg 317, 071-325-4425)
7. Place a radio into operation (AN/PRC-77 or AN/PRC-119) and troubleshoot. (TM 5820-890-10-1, Sec. II-III, and TM 5820-627-12, with changes 1,2 and 3)
8. Send a radio message (STP 21-1 SMCT, pg 47, 113-571-1016)
9. Encode and decode messages using KTC 600 Tactical Operations Code (STP 7-11BCHM14-SM-TG, pg 3-454, 113-573-4003)
10. Use night vision devices (AN/PVS-4's, 7's and unaided night vision)

The Ranger Stakes provide the RIs an opportunity to evaluate individual competency and to correct deficiencies on the spot. Those who fail a task are retrained immediately and retested. To continue the course, seven of the ten tasks must be successfully completed on the first or second try. Those failing to meet the standard are disenrolled from the course or recycled into the next class.

In an area outside of Camp Rogers, the students take their land navigation test...both day and night. Ranger candidates are only authorized one compass of military issue to run the land navigation course. Those students found with an additional or non-issue compass, such as an orienteering compass, will be dropped from the course. Any student who fails the day or night land navigation course will be retested. Those who fail a second time will be disenrolled or recycled. Day 5 of RAP completes this segment of training...which is topped off with a 12-mile tactical foot march at a minimum rate of 15 minutes per mile with either a 40-pound rucksack in the winter or a 35-pound rucksack in the summer.

Each day of this assessment period involves a great deal of physical training...whether it be a pre-dawn run or hours of hand-to-hand combat. When a soldier confronts an enemy "up close and personal"...particularly if the soldier is unarmed, the winner of such a meeting engagement will most likely be the one who reacts first, with as much deadly force as possible. Thus, the need for hand-to-hand combat.

Hand-to-hand combat is performed in pairs, where the students learn the basics of how to use their fists, elbows, knees, feet, and even heads to disable an opponent. Boxing is also a part of the program, which includes several progressive classes of boxing instruction. Eventually, all Ranger students will be paired off...IAW height and experience...for a 15-second bout to be fought within a 12-by-12-foot ring. The ring is small enough to force "eyeball to eyeball" contact and the session, while short to minimize potential injuries, is long enough to give each student a taste of what it's like to confront an enemy with only one's hands.

Despite the garrison environment, complete with barracks and mess hall, many of those who fail, do so during this preliminary phase. For those who successfully complete RAP, the second portion of the Benning phase is conducted at Camp Darby, a facility with few permanent structures. Located deep in the wooded hills of Benning, the Ranger students train, eat, and sleep in the open. It is here, in heavily forested terrain, that the Ranger Student is introduced to the patrolling techniques that will allow the RI to assess the candidate's leadership abilities under stressful field conditions.

The Darby portion commences with an airborne assault for those qualified. 'Leg' students—sorry, I had to say it, though I must sadly admit that I, too, was once a leg Ranger—are trucked. The students assemble in a clearing near the camp's headquarters and begin three days of intense classroom instruction on patrolling fundamentals, advanced land navigation techniques, troop leading procedures (TLP), battle drills, and leadership responsibilities. PT and runs are still conducted each morning.

Day four of Camp Darby commences with the students assaulting the Darby Queen obstacle course. Consisting of twenty obstacles emplaced along a densely wooded hillside, the Darby Queen tests each student's endurance, tenacity, and dedication. Crawling, jumping, sliding, and climbing, through, over, and around obstacles, each Ranger negotiates the course with his Ranger Buddy. Assisting each other along the way, the buddy's complete the course as a team, or they do not complete it at all.

Later that afternoon following the Darby Queen, the students engage in survival training. This training will teach them how to catch, prepare, and cook rabbits, chickens, and fish. Usually, the students are not fed anything earlier in the day so after the arduous physical workout of the Darby Queen, it takes little motivation for a Ranger Student to kill and eat his meal for the day.

With the basic training, the Darby Queen, and survival training out of the way, the remainder of the student's time at Camp Darby is devoted to field training exercises focusing on reconnaissance operations. Utilizing the crawl, walk, and run method of training, the RIs first demonstrate and guide the students through the task prior to conducting a field training exercise for grade. The graded exercises are squad level missions. Issuing Operations Orders to conduct day or night reconnaissance missions during the final four days of this phase, students attempt to accomplish the mission against an opposing force (OPFOR) that is determined to "kill" or capture them. As an additional incentive against capture, the OPFOR maintains and operates a prisoner of war compound that is as realistic as peacetime constraints allow. The bottom line here is don't get caught!

\*\*\*\*\*

Prior to 1991, Ranger Classes did not have a five-day RAP. Thus, for us, the pressure was started on Day 1.

\*\*\*\*\*

## 3 JUNE 1980 (R DAY: Day 1)

I hold it to be one of the simplest truths of war that the thing which enables an infantry soldier to keep going with his weapons is the near presence or the presumed presence of a comrade.

Brigadier General S. L. A. Marshall,
MEN AGAINST FIRE, 1947

HARMONY CHURCH (Ranger encampment)

Here it is, the evening of Day One of Ranger Class 10-80. "The best of men, Ranger Class 10!" Hoo, ahh! I'm sitting in a classroom undergoing a briefing from the Ranger Senior Tactical Officer. This guy is gung-ho; Airborne Ranger, German Jump Wings, CIB, the works. Hanging above and behind him is a large replica of what we are striving for: The Coveted Black and Gold!

The day hasn't gone too badly. Arrived at 1500, some in-processing and drawing of equipment. Ate a bagged dinner literally on the run. I was assigned to 3rd Platoon, 2nd Squad. There's one Ranger Company here, the 3rd. It's within a barbed wire enclosed compound. There are 163 students starting in our class. We'll see how many finish. Nearly all ranks are here; a major, captains, 1LTs, 2LTs, SFCs, SSGs, and even a few Ranger privates. There are also six officers from Zaire. We were to later find out that some of them were combat veterans who had already participated in a number of operations, to include a battalion sized ambush of an enemy company (+) sized unit—probably Cuban.

It's much easier coming here as a group. The camaraderie of knowing each other has greatly reduced the impact of reporting in. It seems that way for most of the cadets. Four years of prior service for me doesn't hurt either.

Of great concern to me right now is acclimation. It seems that most of my USMA classmates have adjusted to the heat and humidity. I seem to have adjusted also, but it struck me as we were sitting in some bleachers, that I was drenched in sweat while everyone else around me appeared to be dry. Interesting. I have no symptoms of being a heat casualty. Supposedly, as long as you're sweating, you're doing fine. Well, I'm certainly doing enough of that. Hopefully, it will tone down a bit. I'm tired of being soaked all the time.

SLEEP: 040030-040300 (Date/Time Group)    TOTAL: 2.5 Hours
                                          Missed Meals: none
                                          B: Breakfast
                                          L: Lunch
                                          D: Dinner

## 4 JUNE 1980 (Benning Phase: Day 2)

**Cowards die many times before their deaths; the valiant never taste of death but once.**

William Shakespeare,
JULIUS CAESAR, Act II (1599)

Damn! What a welcome. The Morgan team has greeted us in style. We thought we were supposed to start the day at 0400 with a two-mile run and some PT. Our fireguard was going to wake us up at 0330 so we could be properly prepared. Boy, were we caught with our pants down. And I mean that literally. Those RIs came roaring in here at 0300 and blew our stuff away.

I awoke with a start, the lights in my eyes, Rangers running around in a daze bumping into lockers, falling on the floor, and attempting to obtain some semblance of a uniform.

My feet are beat up pretty badly from breaking in my new jungle boots during land nav when we first arrived at Benning. Not a very smart idea, I might add. Blisters, cuts, and open sores galore on both heels. I've never had them hurt this badly before. Great timing. I wanted an opportunity to bandage my wounds and to put my boots and socks on snugly, but that idea literally went out the door with the first flying bodies.

I must admit, though, that I was up to the task. Well, almost, that is. I was awake in an instant and jumped from my bed—the top bunk—in a perfectly executed parachute-landing fall (PLF) right into my locker. Fortunately, I had my fatigue pants on so I didn't have to search blindly for them. While staggering out of the barracks, I stopped to lace up my boots. This proved to be a significant tactical error for I was immediately set upon by two huge RIs. But, I thought what the hell, the worst they could do was kill me. Right?

In formation, the RIs proceeded to place us in the front leaning rest. For those of us needing to finish lacing our boots, which was most of us, we had to lie on our backs and complete the task to the tune of "Get your feet up, get your feet up!"

After a few minutes, those who were missing parts of their uniform were given three minutes to get the missing articles and return. I left to finish lacing my boots. Of course, Mother Nature wanted to get in on the action, also, so I went to the latrine. An RI ambushed me and whispered sweet nothings into my ear as I stood at the urinal taking care of business. By this time, the novelty and shock had completely worn off and, as I had hoped, nothing came of the incident.

Forming up again under the motivational guidance of the RIs, we staggered to the obstacle course where we placed our shirts on the ground and, sans T-shirt, commenced a two-mile run at an easy pace. Damn. The darn feet hurt so.

Returning from the run, we hit the obstacle course where the fun really began. I could hear the thought resonate in the RI's minds: "Let the games begin." Pull-ups first, then a low crawl under very low barbed wire—and lots of it. That wouldn't have been too bad if there hadn't been a foot of mud and water under the wire. That damn course seemed to be 50 yards long and we navigated it on our fronts and on our backs.

Fortunately, we had put our shirts on prior to starting. I must have ended up with at least a half ton of gravel in my pockets.

Next, we negotiated a vertical log climb then the inverted crawl with more mud followed by ropes, about 30 feet high, that hung over a huge ditch that was four-and-a-half feet deep and filled with more water, naturally. Once completed, we double-timed in place before running the circuit again. As luck would have it, the horn blew signaling recall, and I only had to do the rope twice. What a pity.

We double-timed back to the company area, sprayed ourselves down outside of the barracks with a hose, put on a clean uniform, and formed for breakfast. Our first here. Another ritual. Each Ranger has a Ranger Buddy (RB), and each two-man buddy team is supposed to be inseparable. Fortune smiled my way. I have mostly an all-cadet squad and, thus, the law of probability provided me with a cadet for my RB.

Each Ranger does pull-ups first and then reports to the mess hall. There, you and your Ranger Buddy bang through the door yelling and screaming and report to the RI headcount. "Sir, Ranger Lock, roster number 120, second squad, third platoon!" After your RB does the same, the RI inspects and either tells you to eat or throws your sorry carcass out of the mess hall to the end of the line to try it again.

Once in the mess hall, a Ranger can get basically all he wants to eat, but he must eat all he gets. There's a guard at the turn-in point for that. All meals are eaten quickly and silently. Returning to the barracks after a meal is the one time you do not have to double time. You can walk.

There is a Ranger student chain of command and I sure pity them. The RIs show no mercy for tying up, and with our motley crew right now, that's all that happens.

Almost forgot. After the run this morning, a cadet quit the course. The first hour! Seems he was forced to crawl from the worm pit all the way back to the barracks on his stomach after he fell out of the run. It really wasn't that far—the run or the crawl. The most amazing fact is that he had been assigned to a Ranger Battalion as an enlisted soldier and some of the NCO RIs knew him from that assignment. One thing is for certain, though, and that is he will never see this course again having been dropped for Lack of Motivation (LOM).

We had a Ranger demo this morning: hand-to-hand, rappelling, airmobile, and explosives for the finale. An RI came down the slide for life and dropped into the water just as a 100-foot strip of explosives was detonated next to where he dropped. Must admit it was somewhat impressive.

Afterwards, Colonel Cameron, commander of the Ranger Department, talked to us. He alluded to the cadet who quit and traced his family lineage in less than complementary terms. Our Ranger Tac Officer (there is also a Ranger Tac NCO), a 1LT, said that the cadet had suffered an MWA—Massive Wimp Attack. The cadre do not feel too kindly towards our cadet. I wonder why? His resignation has proven to be a bit embarrassing for us, his USMA classmates. What of the Long Gray Line?

There isn't much else to say at this time. It's 1400 and we're at the Personnel Office taking care of our records. We cadets have already had most of everything done for us paperwork wise so we're not doing much of anything. I hadn't realized it, but there are about sixty officers in this class. After this respite, it'll be back to the barracks for the legs and jump refresher training for the airborne.

Other than the morning, the day's proven to be relatively slow for us legs, especially having from 1500-1730 off to work on TA-50 and cat eyes for our patrol caps (PC) while the airborne were gone for jump-refresher.

Each group, officers, enlisted, and cadets were taken separately to the Tac office to verify their social security numbers and names. Our Tacs said the cadets were the most motivated of all. While we waited around, we entertained the RIs. Ended up having fun playing charades with a sexual theme.

It's now 2000. Dinner's over and we're standing inspection. Got tagged as a server for dinner. Bad timing. Should have eaten slower. No problem, though. Everyone ate well—I served the main course— though the mess steward was not a happy camper that I used up so much meat.

Well it's now official. Another Ranger's gone and it's been barely 24 hours. This guy was in our platoon and in my bay. There's supposed to be a third leaving, also, so the Tac NCO said. He gave us a little pep talk on quitting. Must admit, it's a bit of a paradox. On one hand, the Ranger Cadre want to run the wimps out. On the other hand, they state privately "Don't quit. Give it a chance." Bottom line is it's psychological warfare. Those with the desire, tenacity, and dedication will stick it out no matter what.

Three formations tonight to see how quickly we could spring from our bunks and form on the company street. We got it down to a minute and half by staying out of our bunks and hanging out in the doorway.

SLEEP: 042330—050330              TOTAL: 4 Hours

                                             Missed Meals: none

## 5 JUNE 1980 (Benning Phase: Day 3)

> **Morale is a state of mind. It is steadfastness and courage and hope. It is confidence and zeal and loyalty. It is élan, esprit de corps and determination. It is staying power, the spirit which endures to the end—the will to win. With it all things are possible, without it everything else, planning, preparation, production, count for naught.**
>
> General of the Army George C. Marshall,
> 15 June 1941, address at Trinity College,
> Hartford, Connecticut

The hand-to-hand pit at 0330 hours this morning. Two hours worth of fun. Falls, basic fighting stance, hip throws. The Morgan Team was not very demanding today, all things considered. Luckily, I was able to keep myself pretty clean. No sawdust down my back or pants. How I hate spray downs at the pit in the morning. All it does is wet us down enough to allow for the sawdust to stick to our bodies better.

We double-timed back to the barracks, stripped down, and sprayed ourselves off with the hose. No shower. With some form of PT every morning, the proper cleaning of this uniform is indispensable. Things are funky enough without having to wear a nasty uniform at the start of each day. I would love an opportunity to wash these fatigues but, instead, I just go into the latrine, rinse them in a big sink, squeeze most of the dirt and grime out, then hang them outside on a line. In the 95+ degree heat, they dry very quickly and are even bearable to wear the next day to PT.

During the day, we had a two-and-a-half-hour class on communications procedures (CEOI), identification of friendly and enemy vehicles, electronic counter measures (ECM), the Threat (Soviet tactics), etc., etc., etc. Afterwards, off to demolition: TNT, C4, and dynamite. We seemed to spend more time in the front leaning rest today than we did with the demolition.

After dinner, we picked up our weapons. We seem to have a pretty good squad, to include four officers. One of them is a turn-back. He had an upper respiratory infection and during the five-mile Ranger run he had to stop and spit out mucus. They considered that a fallout—which you cannot do on that particular Ranger run. He was a No-Go at that 'station' and, consequently, recycled to our class.

It's now 2300 and man, what a night. At 2145 hours, the Tac NCO said we were to be in bed. Our platoon was—the others were not. As a class, we really have to get our act together. We stayed in bed knowing something was going to happen and happen it did.

PT formation at 2200. Then off to the pits. Double-time, pushups, front leaning rest. We'd get down in the front leaning rest and hold that for four to five minutes while the Tac Officer would 'counsel' us. After thirty minutes of this, we returned to the company area where we were held at parade rest for another half hour while the Tacs continued to counsel us—which, I must admit they do very well—for LOM. They call this type of training motivation drills.

That damn company street. Nothing but sharp gray gravel that digs into the palms of your hands as you execute the front leaning rest. We did hundreds of pushups this night. One person dropped, we all dropped. Finally starting to act as one unit and not as 161(-) individuals. One unit. That's what they want. Everyone's voice is hoarse from so much hooting and hollering. The Tac NCO's vocal cords are totally gone. Mine are starting to go. Others can barely cackle.

Right now I'm sitting fireguard. Must admit that to date, this has not been my idea of fun. In the future, I'm not sure how coherent or how long I'm going to be able to write. We've only just begun—sounds like a song—but even now time is becoming less and less free.

The Ranger School uniform policy is rather unique. There is no rank or unit affiliation for Ranger students. Consequently, the only items on your uniform are your nametag, U.S. Army, and any skill badges you may have—such as airborne wings.

As for the condition of the uniform, just about anything goes. The uniforms on the students here run the gamut from new fatigues to uniforms that have been through the course two to three times, such as those worn by students assigned to one of the two Ranger Battalions (note: this being 1980, there were only two Ranger Battalions active). Their uniforms were obtained through their RIP and leave a bit to be desired. One of these RIP Rangers has a pair of fatigue pants that does not have a crotch! There's just a big hole where the cloth used to be. Talk about letting them hang...

SLEEP: 052320—060315 TOTAL: 4 Hours
Missed Meals: none

## 6 JUNE 1980 (Benning Phase: Day 4)

> **In battle, casualties vary directly with the time you are exposed to effective fire. Your own fire reduces the effectiveness and volume of the enemy's fire, while rapidity of attack shortens the time of exposure. A pint of sweat will save a gallon of blood.**
>
> General George S. Patton, Jr.
> WAR AS I KNEW IT, 1947

Normandy anniversary. Hoo Ahh! Three and a half mile run; nine fallouts, one, a cadet, was a heat casualty. I volunteered for cadence calling—proved to be a big mistake when we sprinted for a mile or so. Really sucked it down. A cadet fell in the middle of the formation and took ten Rangers down with him. I had to hurdle over the bodies to keep from joining the crowd. It was a hot run.

Hit the worm pit afterwards. Felt good to lie in the cool mud and water but we have to watch out for the barbed wire. Looking around, I see a multitude of tic-tac-toe X's and O's from the wire etched on many of the shaved heads. This part of training really calls for one to keep his head down.

The morning was pretty busy. We had a late formation by Ranger School standards then went to the classroom for a lecture on health. Later, we had a field class on airborne and airmobile operations, in addition to pacing the land navigation course with the Morgan Team. Rough time. Approximately 100 degrees heat, 99 percent humidity, and approaching 98 percent humility. All running, marching, and outside physical activity were canceled on post. We, of course, are the exception.

The Tac Officer marched us back one-and-a-half miles from training. It was hot. After dinner, we had evening classes on Terrain Analysis. We had a fine time with these Morgan Team members during class. A lot of good jokes. After they finished, the Tac Officer went over more map reading.

Of course, the day could not pass by mistake free. Someone in our platoon apparently picked up the wrong weapon and left it in the second floor bay in the barracks—our platoon area—rather than return the weapon to its owner. Fortunately, we found it, but we could feel the barometer dropping and the storm front was starting to move in.

While everyone else went to sleep at 2350, the Tacs lectured our platoon. The Tac Officer ripped into the 'someone' and applied a number of highly descriptive adjectives to that someone's family lineage. He offered only a minor spot report if the individual fessed up. Right... as if he wouldn't be a marked man from that moment on. No taker. The Tacs kept us up until 0100. Shouldn't complain, it could have been worse.

SLEEP: 070100—070330                    TOTAL: 2.5 Hours
                                        Missed Meals: none

## 7 JUNE 1980 (Benning Phase: Day 5)

> **Confirmation of the ground is of the greatest assistance in battle. Therefore, to estimate the enemy situation and to calculate distances and the degree of difficulty of the terrain so as to control victory are virtues of the superior general. He who fights with full knowledge of these factors is certain to win; he who does not will surely be defeated.**
>
> Sun Tzu,
> THE ART OF WAR, c. 500 BC

Two hours in the Pit. Rinsed off under the showers. Trucked to class on terrain features. Afternoon land nav for record. No sweat, figuratively speaking. There were six points total; four points to pass, five points to max, while the sixth is in event of self-correction while on the course.

It's a jungle out there. Wait-a-minute vines, incredible undergrowth. Stepped on a snake. Found the third point, signed the list hanging from it to verify we were actually there—what, they don't trust us?—then drove on for the fourth.

Unfortunately, it wasn't until I arrived at the fourth that I realized that I had forgotten to write down the third point's number! What an idiot. Had to motor approximately 700 meters back through the brush to get it. Left me with a real case of the butt.

The Morgan Team blew the student commander's doors off at the nav site, along with the rest of the chain-of-command. Many cadets did not fare well. If you bolo the first time, there is one makeup; fail that and you're out. We ended up searching for a missing cadet. Turned out that he was a heat casualty.

My opinion of our USMA liaison officer continues to rise. He gave us a 'poop' (information update) talk during a break. Said we were doing really well despite what everyone else—Morgan Team, Tacs—said. He'll be with us all summer. Definitely a hard worker.

I asked an RI this afternoon about Colonel Elliott Sydnor, the last Ranger School Commandant. I was informed that he just left last week and was sorely missed. It turns out that he left very unexpectedly. Possibly training for a mission into Iran after the embassy hostages. Who knows

This evening the entire chain of command was relieved. Another cadet resigned. I thought we were all hand picked, highly motivated?

SLEEP: 080100—080330                    TOTAL: 2.5 Hours
                                        Missed Meals: none

## 8 JUNE 1980 (Benning Phase: Day 6)

**It is not enough to fight. It is the spirit which we bring to the fight that decides the issue. It is morale that wins the victory.**

General of the Army George C. Marshall,
MILITARY REVIEW

Wake up was at 0330 followed by a good three-and-a-half mile run. Same guy who fell in formation last time crashed and burned again. Wiped out only six Rangers this time. Two guys were kicked out because they dropped out of this, their third run. The RIs took us to the worm pit but it was a psyche. Just as we were ready to jump in and negotiate the muck, we were formed up and moved back to the barracks.

Classes on patrolling all morning from 0630 to 1230. We then spent the afternoon outside with practical exercises. All of these classes were conducted by the Morgan Team.

After dinner, we moved back to the shed for a talk by the Tacs. They discussed the relief of the chain-of-command the other day. The Tacs are clearly annoyed that the company is not pulling together. They talked about cooperation—cooperate and graduate. This is their second talk on this subject matter.

We could have done a hell of a lot worse for Tacs. We ended up doing all sorts of crazy antics to include pushups and the 'dead cockroach.' What is the dead cockroach, you ask? It's a favorite of the RIs. You find yourself a nice graveled section, lie on your back, and place both your legs and arms fully extended over your body. Combine that position with some motivational 'hymns' led by the RIs and you'll find yourself having a hell of a party. Contrary to previous experiences, this session actually proved to be somewhat entertaining and enjoyable. Pretty sick, huh?

Our USMA liaison officer talked to us again during a break. Helps to see him around—a contact with the outside world we no longer have direct contact with.

SLEEP: 082230—090330          TOTAL: 5 Hours
                                     Missed Meals: none

## 9 JUNE 1980 (Benning Phase: Day 7)

> **As for the soldiers, all you can do is to imbue them with esprit de corps, in other words the conviction that their regiment is better than all the other regiments in the universe.**
>
> Frederick the Great,
> TESTAMENT POLITIQUE, 1768

Not much activity today. Up at 0330 for two hours of hand-to-hand. After breakfast, classes until the afternoon. After a quick lunch of C-rats—the precursor to the three lies in three letters Meal, Ready-to-Eat MRE, we ran practical exercises on patrolling techniques.

I received a minor spot report during dinner for having an ice cream—one of life's critical basic food groups, you know. Ice cream can be a real life or death situation for a Ranger student. The ice cream is kept in a freezer in the seating area of the mess hall. The Tac NCO said that he had told us no more ice cream. I told him that he had only threatened to take away this 'privilege.' He was rather upset with me for contradicting him. "The Ranger Instructor is always right even when wrong," that is Ranger Law #2. What is Ranger Law #1? "An RI is never wrong," of course. Oh well, didn't win that skirmish, and it wasn't even worth the effort to fight the battle. I have to learn to just smile, keep my mouth shut, and drive on.

The weather was not too bad today. It must be ten degrees cooler and there is a breeze—so nice. This evening, the company was reorganized. I moved from 2nd squad, 3rd platoon to 3rd squad, 4th platoon which included JC, Mac, and three of the officers from Zaire. I also linked up with a new Ranger Buddy.

We only had cold water in the old billets. We thought that was part of the training. Turns out everyone else but us had hot water. Damn. Talk about getting the shaft.

Fourth platoon has only three squads. Therefore, 3rd squad is upstairs by itself. Plenty of room and clean, not funky. Only problem is this squad fights with itself. There is so little cooperation between anyone other than JC, Mac, and myself.

The Z monster—the beast of sleep—was rampant, again, in class today. The 'Moto' rock, a twenty-five to thirty pound rock...or so it seemed...that is held overhead by Rangers found sleeping in class, saw a lot of action.

At 2130 hours, another company formation. We're highly unmotivated and uncooperative, therefore, it was the front leaning rest and dying cockroach positions for us. That damn street has more dust and rocks than I've ever seen in one place. No doubt in my mind that it is intentional. I thought this form of torture would have been outlawed as unconstitutional under the heading of cruel and unusual punishment.

SLEEP: 100001—100330                     TOTAL: 3.5 Hours
                                          Missed Meals: none

## 10 JUNE 1980 (Benning Phase: Day 8)

> **The main thing is always to have a plan; if it is not the best plan, it is at least better than no plan at all.**
> General Sir John Moash,
> 1918 letter

We ran our last run until the Ranger five miler. We even saw the last of the worm pit—forever. Damn pebbles and gravel in the low crawl pit are sharp.

The day is still cool, which is great. Our Ranger class is down to 146 now—17 Rangers have dropped by the wayside to date.

My feet are feeling better; they're actually healing. I've been able to take pretty good care of them. In their place, though, my knee is starting to act up, an old wrestling injury. Feels like it's wrenched but it will hold out.

Classes in the morning. Company started to put on skits. Turns out the RIs love to be entertained. The more creative we are, the more fun they have, the better we are treated. Consequently, we have a 'committee' of classmates who 'write, produce, and perform' shows or skits for their—and our—behalf. Performed during training breaks or between classes, some of these skits turn out to be quite engaging. Today, the caterpillar one proved to be excellent. But, then again, considering who and what we are, our criticism may be a bit biased when one considers our malformed sense of humor.

From 0930–1130, hand-to-hand. That was not fun. As we ran around the pit after a period of training, the RIs called out that the last Rangers to fall in on their equipment would have some additional 'instruction.' I was caught in the pit as one of the last because all of the other SOBs bailed out early and did not complete a full two laps. That will be the last time that happens. Sometimes it seems one must pay the price for following the rules. Ugh... sounds like a whine.

During the afternoon, we spent four hours going over the operation's order (OPORD) format. Later, the RIs from Camp Darby issued one for homework.

Our company still has very little motivation. We returned to the company area after classes and were pounced on by the Tacs. They placed us in the front leaning rest for approximately half an hour. The street is quickly becoming a real pain in the hand.

Got a letter today from my USMA sponsor. Very nice letter and it helped a lot. Another cadet bites the dust—heat and run casualty. Got to bed exceptionally early tonight. Must have been a mistake on the part of the RIs.

SLEEP: 102130—110330                    TOTAL: 6 Hours
                                        Missed Meals: none

## 11 JUNE 1980 (Benning Phase: Day 9)

> Now artillery has changed everything. A cannon ball knocks
> down a man six feet tall just as easily as one who is only
> five feet seven.

Frederick the Great,
A HISTORY OF MY OWN TIMES, 1789

Only one more session of hand-to-hand left. SSG S—an RI—was the NCOIC today. We did pushups and front leaning rest for a major part of the two hours. SSG P—another RI of "elevate your feet on my Georgia pine" fame—was on us throughout the session and took the last Rangers in the pit and ran them during the entire break.

Field Artillery (FA) classes today. The skit during class about Ranger attack dogs was good; the students sic'ed the Tac NCO. As for the tension relief team, their theme was masturbation and it was outstanding. The Rangers huddled together playing the fingers and 'ejaculated' with water. It was worthy of an Emmy.

In the afternoon, we went to the FA range. We had a little call for fire exercise for grade. Afterwards, we went to bunkers down range and called 105mm fire in on ourselves. The artillery fired a final protective fire (FPF) that included 8 inches and 155mm. One of the rounds landed what seemed to be only twenty feet in front of the bunker. Not bad.

After the barrage, we left the bunkers and picked up shell fragments. They were still hot to the touch, jagged, and multi-hued from the intensity of the shell's detonation.

After dinner, we started to pack for Camp Darby where we would practice our patrolling techniques. We're finished with Harmony Church until next Friday. Not a bad evening otherwise. We packed and moved all non-essential items to another billets. We also had to do part of an Operations Order for homework.

Other than that, not much else to do. Wrote two letters; one to Donnie and the other to my USMA sponsor. The company appears to finally be coming together. The skits have helped a lot. Who knows.

There may be hope for us yet. Let's keep our fingers crossed and pray it lasts.

SLEEP: 120200—120400                           TOTAL: 2 Hours

                                                Missed Meals: none

## 12 JUNE 1980 (Benning Phase: Day 10)

**In war nothing is achieved except by calculation. Everything that is not soundly planned in its details yields no result.**

Napoleon,

18 September 1806, to Josephine,

CORRESPONDENCE

The fireguard fell asleep again. Damn. It's the last day and he can't even stay awake for a lousy thirty minutes. But, then again, the lack of sleep is starting to hit us all and it's proving to be exceptionally tough to remain awake at times, especially when sitting. SSG P fell us out early but, to our surprise, he did not drop us.

Off to Darby, where, immediately upon our arrival, we were informed that "time was of the essence." In other words, they were saying "Get your asses off the bus, now!" With duffel bags flying out the bus windows, we did pretty well sounding off as we conducted a mass tactical operation out of every opening on the bus. We were ordered to dump the contents of our duffel bags and rucks out on the ground to be searched for contraband and 'pogie bait'—another term for junk food. The RIs went about their usual chores which resulted in many pairs of boots on trees for elevated pushups.

Everyone was given a tour of Darby—which is not saying much, for there is so little here to start with. While our platoon had an easy time of it, the other platoons were not so lucky. Second platoon had to low crawl with rucks on their backs while first platoon double-timed and did pushups with theirs. How I hated double-timing everywhere at Benning with that ruck.

We had classes in the morning from 1000 to 1200 hours: air drops and air assault. This is the place for planning, where we will learn how to fully develop, coordinate, and deliver Warning and Operations Orders (OPORDs). All in all, the company appears to have made a good first impression. Hope it keeps up.

Our classroom is a pressure cooker. It's a steel enclosed building with parachutes and camouflage netting hanging all over inside. It is steaming in there—I now have an idea as to what a lobster must feel as it's being lowered into the pot.

Right now we're pretty well burnt out. We can hardly keep our eyes open during class, and we haven't even started patrolling yet. It looks like it will be a very, very long summer.

It is 1600 and we're into it now. Patrolling. The planning takes a lot of hard work if you want to meet their standards, which, of course, you do. But it is not as difficult as it seems. While it requires a lot of mental work, a Ranger has unlimited use of his Ranger Handbook. All you have to do is follow its steps and procedures. How can anyone go wrong?

We have a recon patrol slated for tomorrow, and I am the M60 machine gunner. There isn't even a M60 shoulder strap to go with the weapon. No doubt this puppy is going to prove to be quite a burden.

We're supposed to set up a bivouac site tonight, but when, I do not know. We ate chow standing up because we left the area dirty during lunch.

I'm taking pictures clandestinely, and I feel like a spy. If I'm caught, I gather that the RIs will not be very receptive to my journalistic endeavors. It's worth the risk. I have some great shots, I hope.

They've changed our organization again for the third time. We now need three platoons—one airborne, two leg. Not four as we've had. I'm now in 4th squad, 2nd platoon with a fellow prepster and good friend, Ray, the Field Marshall. I refer to him as the Field Marshall because he's a fanatic about the Second World War and should have been a Prussian by birth. We both attended the USMA Preparatory School at Fort Monmouth, New Jersey, the year prior to our acceptance at West Point; hence the title "prepster." There are also nine other cadets in our squad.

We're spending all of our time in a planning bay now. The overhead cover and sand table provided by the bay are a great asset to our planning. Soon, though, we know that these resources, too, will go away.

Received a letter from Donnie today. Good to hear from him. Letters and meals are the only things one can look forward to around here other than pushups and double-timing. Soon, we probably will not even be able to look forward to that, even, as we spend more of our time in the field. We're told there is no mail while you're on patrol unless you have a kind and benevolent RI—a contradiction in terms?—who brings it out during the morning changeover of RIs.

Mail calls are very entertaining. Some families, friends, and girlfriends try to slip pogie in by mail. The RIs inspect everything. If it's a package or a letter that seems to be particularly heavy or bulky, the Ranger student will open it—federal law requires this much at least—in front of the RIs and us. Should there be pogie, the Ranger student will insist that the RIs have some—read that as all—of it. It's enough to make a grown man cry seeing pogie wasted on the unappreciative. One of my own letters even fell prey to an RI inspection. It turned out that my sister had tried to slip some sticks of Gatorade gum by the ole inspectors. She had taped them flat within the envelop but the weight and rigidness must have led them to believe it was packed with drugs for they had me come forward when they called my name. Opening the letter before them brought a gleam to their eyes, a smile to their faces, and a stream of drool down their chins. Extracting the strips of gum from the letter, I ceremoniously offered each RI a piece. Of course, they did not refuse. Oh well....one can vicariously enjoy I imagine.

We headed back to the company area to pick up our rucks and duffel bags. We didn't get started on our bivouac until 2300. What fun. We had to walk through the woods in the dark to the bivouac site. A harbinger of things to come? Many of us crashed and burned in the dark as we made the trek. It was slow going putting up our pup tents in the middle of the night.

SLEEP: 130001—130400                TOTAL: 4 Hours

                                              Missed Meals: none

## 13 JUNE 1980 (Benning Phase: Day 11)

**When making a plan, try to put yourself in the enemy's mind, and think what course it is least probable he will foresee and forestall. The surest way to success in war is to choose *the course of least expectation*.**

                         Captain Sir Basil Liddell Hart,

                          THOUGHTS ON WAR, 1944

Friday the 13th. Damn. Maybe one of these days I'll be able to chew my food instead of swallowing it whole. We spent most of the morning going over Operations Orders for patrols. They're like nothing we've ever seen before. The RI read one for a twelve-man recon patrol. It lasted for nearly two hours. Sleep deprivation is here to stay. It was the greatest battle of my life just trying to stay awake, though, I have to admit that I lost a few skirmishes and blacked out on my feet from time to time.

Today, we conducted a little recon patrol. Not too bad, only two clicks—one click equals 1 kilometer equals 1K—or so out. I carried the M60 for which I had to use an M16 strap since an M60 strap was unavailable. The strap did some serious carving on my neck.

We patrol with load carrying equipment (LCE), full Special Forces rucks, and weapons. Not exactly a light load. Of course, we are camo'ed up, our sleeves are down, and we wear black gloves. On the way back from the objective, we had a fire fight. I lit them up with 200 rounds from the M60. What a blast—literally and figuratively speaking.

After a very quick dinner, we received our Operations Order. We worked on it in the bay until 2300. I had left my ruck on the cables (1-inch diameter steel cables stretched out in a straight line upon which our unit formations are aligned), as did about forty others. Turns out a

Master Sergeant RI picked them up and we had to see him to get them back. The result will probably be a negative spot report.

As I moved about camp trying to locate my ruck, I note Rangers are low crawling and doing pushups everywhere. I surmise the RIs are just testing our motivation to attain the Coveted Black and Gold.

SLEEP: 132330—140330                    TOTAL: 4 Hours

Missed Meals: L

## 14 JUNE 1980 (Benning Phase: Day 12)

> **One of the greatest difficulties in war is to have the men inured to marching ... The rapidity of a march, or rather skillful marches, almost always determine the success of war ... It is this power of marching which constitutes the strength of infantry; and enterprises which seem to present the greatest difficulties, become comparatively easy by the advantages accruing from rapid marches.**
>
> Marshal of France Michel Ney,
> MEMOIRS OF MARSHALL NEY, 1834

RIs detonated artillery simulators near our camp site at 0330. We didn't have to be in formation on the cables until 0445. Unfortunately, the student chain of command opted to have us form up earlier than necessary. When will they learn? It's a test of our leadership abilities that we continue to fail.

We had a hot A breakfast—that means 'normal' food—and were issued one C-rat to last us until sometime tomorrow. By 1300, we had finished the Warning and Operations Order and moved out to the pickup zone (PZ) for an air assault.

Airmobile at 1700. What a blast. UH-1H Huey helicopters. Twelve patrols departed from the base camp: five airborne, five airmobile, two trucked. My squad loaded aboard the chopper in full combat gear and were inserted about ten minutes later behind "enemy" lines.

This is my first ever air assault. It was a low level flight with plenty of twists and turns. We sat in the doorway with our feet hanging out. All that secured us in the bird was a puny little lap belt. What a rush. It felt as if we were actually going into combat which, I imagine, is the intent.

Our patrol set down on the LZ where we were immediately ambushed. Began to move to the objective after our little firefight. Wouldn't you know that it would rain for the first time since we've been here? We won't be back in until tomorrow morning. Ugh. Being wet is such a nasty feeling.

My patrol consists mostly of cadets. The RIs have told us everything we need to know about patrolling, and we can even use our notes and Ranger Handbook for anything that we do. It's even encouraged. I've really learned quite a bit so far about light infantry tactics.

At this moment, I am part of the recon and surveillance element overwatching our objective, a "Surface-to-Air" (SAM) battery. Our patrol set up our patrol base (PB) in a swamp.

Moved out at 0100 for recon. Couldn't see a damn thing. Moved cross-country, through jungle and streams. I believe the Ranger Department has imported part of deepest, darkest Africa and planted it right here.

SLEEP: none                              TOTAL: 0 Hours
                                         Missed Meals: L

## 15 JUNE 1980 (Benning Phase: Day 13)

**A good solution applied with vigor *now* is better than a perfect solution ten minutes later.**

General George S. Patton, Jr.,
WAR AS I KNEW IT

No breakfast. No sleep. We reconned an objective this morning at 0400. My partner, a cadet, fell asleep while I was out conducting a surveillance of the objective. Upon my return, I couldn't find him.

Back in the perimeter, my fellow Rangers grew concerned as the heavy snores of an obviously sleeping individual began to rise in decibels.

Whispers began to permeate the air as everyone sought to quiet the offender before the RI heard him. Soon, however, it was discovered that it was the RI himself...fast asleep! As he woke, he began to scream for his rifle. Seems that even RIs can feel more than just a bit fatigued and suffer flashbacks.

Finally coherent, the RI quickly noted that my partner wasn't with me and underwent loss of coolant and began a nuclear meltdown. He yelled out the Ranger's name four times but received no response in return. The RI then turned on a flashlight and found our lost Ranger lying face down with his arms by his side approximately two feet away from where we were standing. The RI screamed the cadet's name into his ear. The Ranger's head popped up and the first thing out of his mouth was "I'm not sleeping, RI!" A Pavlovian response, I'm sure. Why hadn't he answered the RI when he called? He had, so claimed the cadet. What ever happened to Duty and Honor? He was a zombie, and it was hilarious—though the cadet was not amused by the major minus spot report he received as a result.

We finished our mission and trucked back in around 0830. The patrol was graded but the RIs say it was not weighted. In other words, it does not count. I passed. Unfortunately, no one else in the patrol did and, besides, it wasn't for record.

They grade very hard at this site—undoubtedly to get our attention. It has to get easier over the next phases for, if it doesn't, no one would pass. There are just too many critical requirements to recall and employ.

The main problem with those who are failing is that they are afraid to take charge, to take command. That's what this entire course is about: Leadership. Even if you don't know what you're doing, do something. In most cases, it will probably accomplish the mission and show that you are not afraid to make a decision. That's what I believe the RIs are looking for.

At 1100, we did the Darby Queen, a 20-obstacle confidence course. With no sleep or food but plenty of hazing from the RIs, who greatly assisted our physical development by taking every opportunity to elevate our feet, the course was a real bear—ropes, logs, cargo nets, and low crawling under plenty of barbed wire. We returned from the Darby

Queen completely soaked and covered from head to foot with sand, the nastiest of feelings.

Finally, we had a chance to take a cold shower; the first in three days. Damn funky uniform and me. Our jungle fatigues dry out quickly and are excellent, all things considered. On patrols, the drying is greatly assisted by the fact most of us do not wear underwear or T-shirts—they just maintain moisture. Be careful, though. If your fatigue pants have zippers, they can prove to be your worst enemy. I speak from personal experience on that one. Oh, the pain!

My jungle boots are finally broken in all the way. About time; they almost broke me. They have the tar—or should that read shoe polish?—knocked out of them. My feet have healed pretty well, though the bottoms are bruised and the heels have not recovered fully. The knee is holding out well, also. All in all, physically fit. Knock on wood. Mentally, no problems either as long as you overlook my warped personality and perverted sense of humor. A full and complete lunch and dinner. Ah, what a relief. I'm stuffed. My stomach must have shrunk somewhat. Ol' Sarge let us off the hook about the unsecured rucks on the cable that night a few evenings ago. No negative spot report. Very lucky, indeed. This afternoon and evening, we planned a combat patrol. Hopefully, it will be rack time soon. Feels like it's been forty-plus hours without sleep. Beam me up, Scotty.

SLEEP: 152115—160345                    TOTAL: 4.5 Hours
                                        Missed Meals: B

## 16 JUNE 1980 (Benning Phase: Day 14)

> **You cannot run a military operation with a committee of staff officers in command. It will be nonsense.**
> Field Marshal Viscount Montgomery of Alamein,
> quoted in de Guingand,
> OPERATION VICTORY, 1947

Pretty easy day today. Ate breakfast at a leisurely pace for once then reported to our bays for final inspection before going on our combat patrol. Last night, another cadet quit. He was my chain-of-command squad leader. Claims to have found religion out here in the woods. That's great, but it doesn't mean he had to quit. Being a Ranger is not exactly synonymous with being a heathen now, is it? Many great military leaders, past and present, are very religious.

Yours truly has now taken his place in the chain-of-command. Ugh! I was looking forward to dinner today but with this additional duty, I can forget about that.

With the mail that has accumulated over the last few days while we were patrolling, I was sure that I'd get at least one letter. There was a boatload of correspondence to be passed out. After the dust settled, the score was everyone else at least 1, Lock: 0. Ah, a big fat goose egg. Mac, alone, got four. This left me somewhat disappointed but, actually, I really shouldn't whimper. I've received five letters since I've been here.

At least some of my humor is still intact, as warped as it may be. It's tempting to quit. But stay focused on the end result. The time will come when it is all over one way or another. What is it they say, "You can make it harder, but you can't make it longer?" Well, no solace in that adage. It doesn't hold any weight here for they can make it longer— can you say recycle?

It's now 2100 and the Operations Order for our combat patrol has just been issued. The patrol has twenty-four Rangers—all cadets—who will be inserted behind enemy lines by airmobile. That makes for some serious problems, for everyone wants to be Chief Mother F..... In Charge (CMFIC), king of the hill. We have already polarized into our little coteries. It's not looking very promising.

SLEEP: 162300—170400                    TOTAL: 5 Hours
                                        Missed Meals: L

## 17 JUNE 1980 (Benning Phase: Day 15)

> **I cannot trust a man to control others who cannot control himself.**
>
> General Robert E. Lee

Finished the Warning and Operations Orders by 1000 hours. Everyone's nerves are beginning to fray, to include mine. One of my classmates made a comment, today, and I snapped. Seems that everyone is an expert on patrolling now, including me, and none of us will listen to anyone else. I shouldn't have lashed out as I did, but I've had a short fuse since yesterday's mail call, and he lit it. Fortunately, I didn't blow all the way. Somehow, I quickly clamped down, shut up, and turned away. That wasn't easy, but it was the best thing to do.

Airmobiled into Cactus Landing Zone again. Still as much fun as the first time. Ambushed again. This time I searched the ambusher's 5-ton cargo truck. I didn't find any food but I did appropriate 100 rounds of 5.56mm. Tough to digest. Maybe a little more salt? Damn, I'm hungry.

Well ... it's now 1900. It was a tough battle, Ma, but we won. Actually, we easily overran the SAM base this afternoon. The only problem was that I wasn't paying much attention to what was going on around me. I was daydreaming about something else when we launched our attack from the assault position. I ran right into a tangle of barbed wire strung along the ground. I ripped my legs up and got three good tears in my jungle fatigue trousers to remind me of my inattentiveness and personal defeat. I even lost an M16 magazine. Overall, not a stellar performance on my part.

During our assault, we fired that objective up so well that we put it on fire, literally. Just beyond the objective we had started a fire with a star cluster. The grass and timber were extremely dry. Other than a few cloud bursts here and there, not much rain in weeks. We tried to put it out, but the wind was blowing and we were getting our butts whipped. Unexpended blanks that had been left lying around were popping all over the place. Sure were an awful lot of them. Since we couldn't stop or contain the fire, we left it. We did call it in, though, so I assume they sent some equipment out to fight the blaze.

Ah. Guess what? Our patrol base is in a swamp again. At least this one isn't quite so bad as the last ones. Now all we need is rain.

SLEEP: none                               TOTAL: 0 Hours
                                          Missed Meals: L

## 18 JUNE 1980 (Benning Phase: Day 16)

**Fatigue makes cowards of us all.**
> General George S. Patton, Jr.,
> WAR AS I KNEW IT

No rain but we've hardly even started patrolling yet and already many of the Rangers are zombies. Everyone crashed when we hit our patrol base last night. The Z monster is a deadly and unmerciful combatant who takes no prisoners, unlike the RIs, who do take prisoners. I believe they do so to have someone to torture. A dead Ranger is no fun to play with.

In the pitch black of night, it took nearly two hours to get our patrol together to move out. I even got nailed by the sleep beast. My security buddy and I sat down in our position to rest and eat. After eating, I let him go to sleep while I took the first guard. That didn't last long. A half hour later, I think I lost it. Where was that high duty concept when I needed it most?

I don't remember very well what happened next. I believe someone came by and tapped me on the shoulder. Why, I don't know—maybe to just get me back on security, but this is normally how we indicate you are the new patrol leader (PL) or assistant patrol leader (APL). My subconscious took over. What a scary thought. I got up, left my equipment, and proceeded to walk around the center of the camp.

I didn't have any idea what I was doing. All I remember was sitting guard one moment and waking up standing in the middle of the patrol base the next. It was all a fog. I was saying something but

I don't recall what it was that I was muttering. I couldn't even remember where I was. At first, I thought that everyone was leaving. I didn't know where my position, partner, or equipment were. Somehow, through some homing instinct—or was it quite simply God taking pity on this poor excuse for a Ranger?—I stumbled across my buddy who was still in a deep sleep. Everyone is doing crazy stuff, and it's only just begun.

Shortly after finding my position, we moved out cross country through a swamp. Vines, thorns, roots, streams, and knee-deep mud. We ended up being three hours late for our 0300 ambush.

After the ambush, we ripped our way through another swamp that was much worse than the first. We had to make our own trail in that we were somewhat "off the beaten path," as the saying goes. I ended up carrying another Ranger's ruck as he had to return to the ambush site for some lost equipment.

During our movement, everyone else missed seeing the three-foot snake curled up in the branch of a tree we were moving through. It was only one foot away, about eye level and didn't appear to be bothered a bit as we made eye contact. Nice.

We established a landing zone and lifted off at 0715. I could have sworn that we were in Vietnam—it looked so much like newsreel clips I've seen. The rest of the day was easy—shower, clean clothes, lunch, and mail. At least my sister wrote. That salvaged some of the day.

Two short classes during the afternoon. The rest of the time was ours. First free time since we've been here. I finished the letter to Donnie's mother. After dinner—less and less food nowadays, we received an Operations Order. Tomorrow is a graded patrol.

SLEEP: 182300—190400                    TOTAL: 5 Hours
                                        Missed Meals: B

## 19 JUNE 1980 (Benning Phase: Day 17)

**... for idleness makes the body soft and weak, while relax-**

ation makes the soul cowardly and worthless; since plea-
sures capturing the passions by enticement of daily habit,
corrupt even the most courageous man. For this reason,
the soldier must never be without occupation.

Onasander,
THE GENERAL, AD58

It's 1900. We're in a swamp, belly down. Oh my aching back. Our
meals are getting smaller and smaller. Today, they cut out cereal and
sweet rolls. How un-American.

Broke down our bivouac site this morning. Won't be needing that
any more, for tonight will be our last night here. Got a hardass, strictly
by the book, SFC RI for a grader on today's patrol that's for record.
Trucked to our departure point this time. It's been pouring on and off
throughout the day, but we've been fortunate in that we've been in the
planning bay during those rainy times.

After crossing the Line of Departure (LD), we navigated through a
swamp. This has been the best one so far because of all the rain. Muck
and slime everywhere. Walked—or should I say waded—through goo
that reached past our knees. At one point, the Ranger in front of me,
who was carrying the M60, fell about three feet off a log that we were
using to cross over a creek. He sank to his hips and couldn't move. I
had to perform an acrobatic act by holding his M60 in one hand and
pulling him out with the other while balancing on the log. It took two
to three minutes to accomplish this. I sure as hell did not wish to go in
there. Nasty funk.

The Field Marshall was the patrol leader and he set our objective
rallying point (ORP) too close to the road. We stopped and settled
down for a stay. I told him that we should pick up and move back 300–
400 meters for security but he elected to remain in place. Later I was
to find out that the paceman had told him we'd traveled 1,300 meters
to my count of 1,800. He opted to go with the 1,300 since the other
Ranger was the "appointed" paceman. So much for classmate loyalties.
Thanks...buddy.

Shortly thereafter, I was designated patrol leader. Lucky me. My first decision should have been to move the objective rally point back just as I had recommended. But did I? No. I was a bleeding heart and decided not to bother my classmates with a move. Because of that, my security was off—at least according to the RI. Proved to be the only thing wrong out of all the tasks that one has to perform as a patrol leader which was enough to fail the patrol. Ah. I knew better. Damn! What an idiot. Supposedly, only about 20 percent of the people pass their graded patrol here. At least I'm with the majority.

At the moment, we are in another swamp searching for another patrol base. Needless to say, this is proving to be somewhat of a bad habit. I want to eat, sleep, and be Mary—or Judy or Leslie or ... for the rest of my days. Only 48 hours until our break. That's the only thing we're living for right now. To be clean and eat food are the only two thoughts on my mind now. Pizza, steak, beer, pretzels, ice cream and strawberries. Oh, just the thought of it hurts.

Marched all night. The Field Marshall and I were a security team during the movement. Kept ourselves awake by asking each other trivia questions on World War II. Pretty demented, huh? For some reason, we weren't very tired.

SLEEP: none                                      TOTAL: 0 Hours
                                                 Missed Meals: L

## 20 JUNE 1980 (Benning Phase: Day 18)

**No operation of war is more critical than a night march.**
Sir Winston Churchill,
THE RIVER WAR, 1899

The last day out and the RIs made the most of it. This was one longgggg patrol. At midnight, we left the patrol base for our final objective, which was only two clicks away. But, traveling cross country through unfamiliar territory in pitch black, is not my idea of fun. I'm sure the intent of this patrol was for Darby to leave us with one last loving memory, for our movement ended up going through 500 meters of pure black, bona fide swamp. Ah. Now, this was the epitome of an excellent gunky, funky, gooey Georgian swamp—vines, roots, trenches, snakes—everything anyone could want in a swamp. I had the PRC77 radio with me. The additional 21 pounds did wonders for my shoulders and back. Whereas everyone else was only sinking into the muck up to their knees, I was fortunate enough to cool myself off by sinking to my thighs. Whew ... was it ever a long haul—about 10 hours worth.

Hitting the objective was a fiasco. The recon party walked right onto it. By this time, it was approximately 0400 hours and, of course, things continued to go wrong. One of the Rangers lost the eyepiece to the AN/PVS-2 Night Vision device. If it hadn't been found during the ensuing administrative search, we probably would have been out there all day Saturday during our break looking for it.

Our jaunt back to the Forward Friendly Lines (FFL) seemed very long, though it was only a bit over two clicks. Back at Darby by 0730, we turned in equipment, debriefed, showered—ah, only the third since we've been out here—and packed. On the cables, the RIs shook us down again. This time for pyrotechnics. They ripped everything apart. By 1230 hours, we departed by bus to Harmony Church. No more Darby.

At Harmony Church, we ate a bagged lunch. We had tests in the afternoon that consisted of inspection, air resupply, land navigation, Friendly Forward Unit (FFU) activities, and radio procedures. Critical tasks had to be passed. If you receive a No Go in any of them, you will be recycled or bounced from the course. Unfortunately, some students failed. One Ranger who failed commo was a recycle from the previous class because he had failed the same task last cycle. Now, with this No Go, he was terminated from the course.

After dinner, the Ranger Tacs took the entire company to get a haircut at the nearby mini PX—even though we felt we did not need one. We spent three hours there. While a few bodies at a time went in for their haircuts, the rest of us were reacquainted with the front leaning rest

Right now it's 2100 hours. I haven't had any sleep in 41 hours. We did have a good dinner, though, and Donnie and his family wrote.

Their support helps a lot.

SLEEP: 202300—210330 TOTAL: 4.5 Hours

Missed Meals: B

## 21 JUNE 1980 (Benning Phase: Day 19)

**Truly then, it is killing men with kindness not to insist upon physical standards during training which will give them a maximum fitness for the extraordinary stresses of campaigning in war.**

Brigadier General S.L.A. Marshall,

MEN AGAINST FIRE

Busy morning. At 0400, we ran our five-mile Ranger run. Not too bad a pace—easy, as a matter of fact. Wasn't winded, but the legs did hurt. We started the run with 144 bodies; 143 finished. The one Ranger fell out at the last turn, 100 feet from the end.

The most difficult thing about the runs is that no one knows the route, therefore, one does not know where or when it will finish. Periodically, the RIs throw a psyche at us. They stop the run in the vicinity of the company area and just when we think it's safe to shift down into a neutral mode, the RIs start running for a couple of hundred yards more. Sometimes, it is very tough to kick start the ol' motor again. That's what happened to our fallout on the five miler.

After breakfast, the confidence course at Victory Pond: log walk, rope drop, suspension traverse, combat survival swim. If you cannot swim with a combat load, you're a No Go—one of those critical tasks you have to successfully complete to be a Ranger.

I upset an RI because I did not drop off the suspension traverse—otherwise known as the slide for life—when he ordered me to. I couldn't see his command; my feet blocked the view. He ended up having me elevate my feet and do underwater pushups.

Finished with the confidence course, we headed off to the pits for hand-to-hand. It was the final one for King of the Pits. Literally threw that one; wasn't taking any chance on getting hurt. Trying to be king is a foolish risk at this point. The objective is the Tab, not a worthless title.

Finally, at 1500, we were on break for eight hours. We were beginning to believe we wouldn't have one. We cadets chartered a bus, dropped our clothes off to be washed—give those cleaners hazardous duty pay and Decon kits, and then went to the PX, Ranger Joe's, and various eating establishments. Procured candy, hamburgers, pizza, soda, beer, and ice cream sundaes. Ah ... this is the life.

Returned for taps formation at 2300. Today is the first day since we've been at Benning that it's rained steadily for more than a half hour. Figures.

SLEEP: 212345—220415                    TOTAL: 4.5 Hours
                                        Missed Meals: none

*****

## ONE PHASE DOWN; TWO TO GO

*****

# BENNING PHASE

*R-Day minus 3. Ranger Haircuts. Note the white skullcap.*

*The company street that left such a lasting impression on our psyche ... and on the palms of our hands.*

*Our Harmony Church classroom. Inside dwelled the dreaded 'Moto Rock.'*

*"Sir, Ranger Lock, roster number one-two-zero, second squad, third platoon." The only words I would utter in the mess hall.*

*After a session in the hand-to-hand pit, an opportunity to cool down with a rinse under the showers. If lucky, one can even get most of the sawdust off his body.*

*Practice patrols at Darby. A very mild and deceptive precursor of things to come.*

*Victory Pond. First one must successfully negotiate the log walk and the Ranger crawl along a horizontal rope.*

*Then it's the slide for life. Make sure you don't raise your feet too high, though, or you will miss the RI's signal to drop.*

*And just when you thought it was safe to hang out after completing the course, you're provided with another opportunity to excel by elevating your feet and knocking out a few dozen pushups.*

# CHAPTER 5

# RANGER SCHOOL: DESERT PHASE

Being barren, the desert cannot be conquered by armies.
Of itself, as Winston Churchill once wrote, the desert yields
nothing to them but hardship and suffocation. The arena
is suitable for nothing except primordial combat, with death
and survival as the issue.

Brigadier General S.L.A. Marshall,
'The Desert: It's Different', INFANTRY, Dec. 1970

From 1983 to 1995, an approximate sixteen-day Desert Phase at Dugway Proving Grounds, Utah, or at Fort Bliss, Texas, was included as one phase of a four-phased Ranger School program. Run by the 7th Ranger Training Battalion, the phase commenced with an in-flight rigging and airborne assault—or an air assault landing by non airborne personnel, onto an objective.

Following the mission, the students moved into a cantonment area. Remaining in garrison for five days, they then received classes on desert-survival techniques to include water procurement and water preservation. Leadership responsibilities, standing operating procedures (SOPs), reconnaissance, and ambush techniques were also reviewed. Additional emphasis was placed on battle drills to include react to enemy contact, react to indirect fire, and react to near and far ambushes. Drills on how to breach barbed and concertina wire with wire cutters and assault ladders were taught as were techniques on how to clear a trench line and how to assault a fortified bunker.

The remainder of the desert training was the actual conduct of field training exercises. Carrying out reconnaissance, raid, or ambush missions, the students moved to the objective by parachute, air assault, or on foot. The phase culminated with an airborne assault—with non-airborne trucked—by the entire class on a joint objective. Soon after, it was back to Ft. Benning.

\*\*\*\*\*

NOTE: Our 1980 class did not have a Desert Phase

\*\*\*\*\*

# CHAPTER 6

# RANGER SCHOOL: MOUNTAIN PHASE

MAXIM XIV—Among mountains, a great number of positions are always to be found very strong in themselves, and which it is dangerous to attack. The character of this mode of warfare consists in occupying camps on the flanks or in the rear of the enemy, leaving him only the alternative of abandoning his position without fighting, to take another in the rear, or to descend from it in order to attack you. In mountain warfare, the assailant has always the disadvantage.

Napoleon,
THE MILITARY MAXIMS OF
NAPOLEON

The 5th Ranger Training Battalion operates the mountain phase which is twenty-one days long and is subdivided into four sub phases: lower and upper mountaineering, mountain techniques, and tactical operations. Here, students will negotiate mountainous terrain, conduct day and nighttime repelling, build rope bridges, and move cross-country conducting day and night combat missions.

After arriving at Camp Frank D. Merrill, the students are assigned 'hootches' within the garrison cantonment with one squad per hootch (note: these facilities are no longer used to billet students). While in garrison, PT is continued with runs of various distances. The first three days are spent within the camp area learning how to tie knots to secure ropes and climbing equipment for mountain operations and how to secure and anchor their rappelling lines. Basic rappelling skills, such as rope handling and belaying are also taught prior to each student's initial rappel down a 20-foot wall of wooden slats.

Moving out of the cantonment area on the fourth day, the students tackle a sixty-foot cliff where they learn how to individually rappel with and without rucksacks. More advanced rappelling techniques include buddy rappelling with an "injured" comrade strapped to the back and a stretcher assist rappel where two Rangers assist a third down the cliff while he is strapped to a stretcher. Successful completion of this part of the course includes passing the knot and belaying test and successfully performing three daytime rappels and a nighttime rappel with rucksack (during the winter months a fixed rope descent may be substituted for the nighttime rappel). Of the three daytime rappels, one must be with rucksack and a second must be accomplished with only two bounds against the cliff.

Following completion of the lower mountaineering phase, it's on to upper mountaineering for Days Five and Six. On top of Mount Yonah, the highest peak in Georgia, students will learn how to conduct free climbs, suspension climbs, and how to use safety lines and mountaineering equipment to climb as well as descend.

The field training exercises commence on Day Eight and involve tactical operations at the platoon and company level. Students conduct the same type of operations as in the past—reconnaissance, ambush, raids, airborne and air assault—but the accomplishment of these missions is much more difficult than at Benning because of the environment in which they have to be performed. Moving along inclines and ridgelines, landing in small drop zones—the smallest being Garrett's Farm at 150 meters by 100 meters with a stream and a Y-shaped band of trees running through the middle of the DZ—and landing zones, makes each mission a serious challenge. There are more injuries in this phase than in any other. Everything from scrapes, bruises, and sprains to more serious injuries such as pulled or torn muscles, dislocations, and broken bones are common occurrences. To successfully complete the mountain phase with the minimum of injuries is a significant accomplishment in and of itself.

## 22 JUNE 1980 (Mountain Phase: Day 20)

> A chaplain visits our company. In a tired voice, he prays for the strength of our arms and for the souls of the men who are to die. We do not consider his denomination. Helmets come off. Catholics, Jews, and Protestants bow their heads and finger their weapons. It is front-line religion: God and the Garand.
>
> Audie Murphy,
> TO HELL AND BACK, 1949

Very, very easy day as far as Ranger School goes. We're still at Ft. Benning preparing for our movement to the mountain camp. Up at 0415, breakfast, critique sheets on Phase One, church, and packing for the rest of the time. Many of us took advantage of the opportunity to go to church. It was nice and cool inside. Looking around, I recalled reading about the many religious converts prior to combat operations. I wonder how many of our class would find religion in the event of hostilities?

Everyone was counseled by the Tac. Seems I've been peered—should I act surprised? Our last action at Darby was to do a peer rating on each member of squad. The school requires that each Ranger peer at least one of his classmates in the top block and one in the bottom block. Normally, as a group, we handle this alphabetically. The Ranger alphabetically ahead is top blocked while the Ranger below is blocked in the bottom. The result is everyone receives a top and a bottom block, and thus, no one would be peered. At least, that's the theory.

I've only been with this squad since the last couple of patrols at Darby. I know very few of the squad members even though most of them are cadets. I went ballistic on them once and let a few of them know exactly what I thought of them, especially our "sleeper." Half of the squad of twelve rated me very well. The other half rated me as the pits. One person rated me a two—on a scale of 1 to 40—while another rated me forty, at the bottom. That bottom one put me under the limit. Needed a total score of 65; got a 63.

Talked with the Tac Officer. I have to learn to be more tactful. For the most part I believe I have, but at the end of our last patrol and after only five hours of sleep out of the last 76—is this beginning to sound a bit like a snivel? I was a little cranky and in a hurry to turn in our equipment at Darby. We were the second patrol to return at 0730 but the very last to get our equipment turned in. That's when I lost it, and that's what did me in on the peers.

I must admit there was a valuable lesson in the peering. Do NOT tell anyone what you think of them until after the peers are complete. Not very bright, Lock, telling them what you really think of them just prior to their filling out peers! Extract your head out of your third point of contact. Fortunately, being peered is not the end. The Ranger Tac indicated that the incident that caused the peering seemed to be an isolated one and he would note it as such. His final recommendation to me was to ensure I engaged my mind next time prior to engaging my mouth. Sound advice, I'd say.

Charlie's gone now. Broke his ankle yesterday while running in the pit. Unfortunate. Lost seven more people on the make-up land nav. All of the cadets passed. Picked up thirteen retreads from mountaineering. Yes, indeed. It was a very easy day. Nothing to do but pack and clean up.

SLEEP: 222300—230300          TOTAL: 4 Hours
                                           Missed Meals: none

## 23 JUNE 1980 (Mountain Phase: Day 21)

**Climate is what you expect but weather is what you get.**

Anonymous

Off to Dahlanoga. Actually, we will be approximately ten miles north of there at Frank Merrill Mountain Camp. Woke up at 0300. Chow at 0400. Cleaned the barracks and boarded commercial buses at 0530. We brought all of our gear from Benning except for that which we stored.

What a change. Weather was rotten for it rained all day. Only the third time, or so, this month. We were soaked, but no problem, for this is almost a day camp in comparison to Benning. No harassment, hazing, or shakedowns; nothing. Our only problem is our student company commander. He's a captain who's been recycled twice. Seems to think his rank means something here. No doubt he'll be peered again. Time will tell.

Each squad moved into its own hooch—a small hut. In the afternoon, we had an admin briefing and some classes on tie downs, commo, and health. The dining facility, a euphemism for Mess Hall, has been designated the best small consolidated dining facility in the Army. Nice atmosphere, excellent food, no rush; we can even talk now. We still do pull-ups before meals, though.

I'm squad leader again, 1st squad, 4th platoon. Another cadet is my Ranger buddy. It's a good squad: seven cadets, five officers. We had the entire evening off after dinner. There's even hot water. Whoopie.

SLEEP: 232200—240400        TOTAL: 6 Hours

Missed Meals: none

## 24 JUNE 1980 (Mountain Phase: Day 22)

**Hygiene ... has such bearing upon the efficiency of armed forces that its place in warfare cannot be denied... The**

> responsibility for the health of crews rests ultimately with
> the commanding officers.
>
> Rear Admiral Alfred Thayer Mahan,
> NAVAL ADMINISTRATION AND WARFARE, 1908

Rained all night and all morning. For once, we were smart. We actually wore rain gear instead of our Ranger poncho—fatigues. We had classes during the morning on recon and patrol base activities.

During the afternoon, we had classes on ambushes and conducted a practical exercise. We ran to the site in LCE with M16s. What a pain. After the demonstration, during which it continued to rain, we ran back. It was mostly uphill and our Ranger Tac Officer tried to smoke us.

Our first mission started this evening. These mission briefings are not nearly as intense as those at Darby. Our RI is a SSG and he seems to be pretty easygoing. Ours even helps during the planning with suggestions. Should be a good patrol.

Not having been in the field for the past four days has allowed us to combat our chiggers, ticks, and cellulite. Everyone was infected with one or the other or all of the above while at Benning. Those darn chiggers burrow under one's skin and inflame the area pretty badly. The more you scratch, the deeper they seem to go. To top it off, it's said that they lay eggs while they are burrowed in there. I've got a number of chiggers on my calves, back, and an arm. Some people are totally covered by these little critters.

The only way to take care of them appears to be by suffocation. We accomplish this by placing finger nail polish over the wound. I use clear but maybe I should change to shocking pink? I've also heard that one way to prevent chiggers is to eat match heads—two to three every four or five days. Something about sulfur in the system. I went a little bit overboard. I "ate" a book of matches over a time period of one day. Talk about stomach cramps. It may have been worth it, though, for I haven't had any new chiggers since.

SLEEP: 242300—250430        TOTAL: 5.5 Hours

Missed Meals: none

## 25 JUNE 1980 (Mountain Phase: Day 23)

> Commanders must remember that ... the issuance of an
> order, or the devising of a plan, is only about 5 percent of
> responsibility of command. The other 95 percent is to
> ensure, by personal observation, or through interposing of
> staff officers that the order is carried out.
>
> General George S. Patton, Jr.,
> MILITARY REVIEW

"Isn't it a great day to be alive and be a Ranger?" the Tac Officer yells. Hell no! I feel like Noah. It's rained now for three days. My squad members were servers today. Rotten deal since it's the morning of our mission, but there were fringe benefits. Some of us appropriated bananas and boxes of cereal. I served coffee cake so you know everyone had plenty of that—to include me. If any of us had been caught, it undoubtedly would have resulted in a big time firing up. But, what the hell, for food...

The camp commander, a lieutenant colonel (LTC), dropped by during our Operations Order. He looked through my ruck and inspected my weapon, an M14, while we briefed. The M14 is an excellent weapon. A new type of stock makes it almost as light as the M16. This rifle feels and fires like a weapon and not like a toy as does the M16.

As soon as we left our planning bay, it started to rain. Great. Conducted rehearsals on the grass airstrip in the pouring rain at 1300 hours. These guys were so gung-ho they even dropped into the prone in an inch or two of water. I was the only one left standing. Looking around, I saw that the RI was watching me. With an "Oh shit," I dropped, to the amusement of the RI and everyone else.

After rehearsals, we trucked to our departure point at 1500. What a Big Freaking Rock (BFR) we humped. This mountain chain is called the TVD for Tennessee Valley Divide. It "be" big all right. We started off in style by crawling up this one mountain that was at least 3,000 feet high with a slope of 45 degrees or more. All of the slopes around here seem to be 45 degrees or more. Did it ever pour at the top of the mountain.

We crawled through the underbrush along a trail that had not been used in quite a while. The leader's recon brought us right out on the objective—not good. We gathered special information requirements (SIR), got fired up and fired up the enemy in return. The M14 fires very well.

At the dissemination of information point, I was made Patrol Leader. I took the patrol along the Appalachian Trail to a working patrol base. There, we established a clandestine patrol base to sleep. Clandestine patrol bases are unique in that the patrol huddles together like a herd of sheep to reduce exposure and signature. Everyone but the Ranger on radio watch can sleep, with the watch being rotated every 30 minutes or so. Unfortunately, there is an entropic movement, a sort of Brownian Motion, that takes effect for one can fall asleep in the center of the herd only to find himself on the outer fringe, freezing, an hour or so later. It had to be the most miserable time anyone's spent yet—cold, wet, tired, hungry, and rain. Ah. It was horrible. We did manage to get most everyone at least three hours of sleep, though. That, in itself, is quite an accomplishment. Most patrols get one hour of sleep, if they're lucky.

SLEEP: 252300—260200 TOTAL: 3 Hours
Missed Meals: L D

## 26 JUNE 1980 (Mountain Phase: Day 24)

> Fear and fatigue impacted on the body in the same way, draining it of energy. That being true, the overloaded soldier became more susceptible to fear; and the more heavily fear began to oppress him, the less strength he had to sustain his burdens. Overloading plus fear—result, mass panic under fire.
>
> Brigadier General S.L.A. Marshall,
> BRINGING UP THE REAR, 1979

Still cold, wet, and miserable. This time many of us are shaking and the teeth are chattering. Better be careful or we'll get major spot reports for noise discipline. Some of us even seem close to developing hypothermia. Where's the hot, June weather when you need it most?

We moved out of the clandestine patrol base for a link-up at 0300. We had to move down a mountain to accomplish this. I took point; an experience I could have done without. Drop-offs, rocks, branches, bushes, and downed trees, as well as darkness, plagued us. Finally, though, we did make it. We linked-up with another squad and moved to establish a patrol base. There, we went administrative for a change of RIs.

During my counseling for this patrol, my RI said that he rarely gives Goes on the first patrol. Must be a first date syndrome. I received one—fortune was smiling my way. Now I'm set for Florida.

While at the patrol base, I changed into a dry and clean uniform. Ah, heaven. It had stopped raining only a few hours before and now the sun was coming out. Since it rarely rains around here, there should be no more rain while in this phase. Let us pray. Also, we got to eat chow—as in C-rats. The feet are beat. They are a nasty white and shriveled up, as are our hands. We look like cadavers.

Patrol base activities aren't too bad. After establishing a patrol base in the early morning hours, there is usually a little respite. Then, prior to the arrival of the new RIs, an event which occurs every day of the patrol, the 'old' RIs conduct an after action review (AAR) of the previous day's activities with the entire patrol. Afterwards, the patrol leaders and assistant patrol leaders are counseled and told whether or not they received a Go.

After the new RIs arrive, there's accountability of equipment and personnel followed by the announcement of a new patrol chain-of-command. He who is tagged as patrol leader then departs with an RI, like a lamb being led to slaughter, to receive a mission brief. The remainder eat, clean up, and sleep—though, not necessarily in that order. This period of time is basically admin.

The rest of the morning and afternoon is devoted to planning, rehearsals, and maintenance. Twenty-five to fifty percent security is maintained. Finally, around 1600 to 1700, we begin the cycle again heading out on a patrol.

Usually, the only change to this routine is if the new RIs have us move to a new patrol base. We don't want to get too comfy now, you know. It could become habit forming.

Our new mission is a combat patrol and, lucky me, I get to pack the M60. We moved out and climbed a bit to a new patrol base. Damn, do my feet ever hurt. Everyone's badly bruised from walking on the sides of their feet and ankles all day and night. At least I'm dry, fed, and in good spirits.

How I could have used some of that excess heat from the other day last night for it was a tad bit cool. Anyway, with the ten million and one dummy and tie down cords attached to my body and equipment, I would be led to believe that there was nothing that could be lost out here except my life. Well, I forgot about Murphy—of anything that can go wrong, will go wrong fame. There was something else to lose: my watch. Damn thing was ripped off last night and disappeared as we were breaking through the brush. Does anyone know what time it is?

Left the patrol base at 1730. Hurt my knee getting up. Locked up on me again—no pun intended. Had to give up the M60 for a while. Halfway up Sassafras Mountain, one of the tallest ones in the chain, I took it again because everyone else was passing it around. The slope of that hill must have been 60 degrees at some points. A long and unnecessary haul. We could have gone around the side of the mountain along the Appalachian trail.

I ran into another snake. This one was a rattler that alerted about two feet away from me. Almost blew him away with the muzzle blast of the M60. Even with blank ammo, that machine gun can spit out some flame. Must admit that it scared the shit out of me when it first rattled, but my reactions were pretty decent. The combat information center within my head apparently was manned—for once—as I nearly shoved the barrel of the 60 down the snake's throat. I was so startled that I barely held off pulling the trigger. I decided to let it keep its seat. What's interesting is that approximately twenty other people passed by, and it did not move. We had just halted, and I suppose it was letting me know that seat was taken. Everyone was opting for the rucksack flop. It's a good thing I held off for a moment. I almost sat on it.

We hit the objective on the other side of the mountain. What a show. Had 400 rounds of blank ammo to fire and wouldn't you know it, the M60 misfired. Damn. Used two 1/4-pound sticks of TNT for demo. We halted on the side of a draw to disseminate information. Actually, it was the side of a cliff. By then, it was 2300 and Rangers were falling asleep all around me. One Ranger's ruck rolled approximately 100 meters down the hill. It would roll ten to twenty meters, seem to stop for a few seconds, then start rolling again. All the while, the Ranger owner was stumbling down the hill after it. Funny as hell. It happened again after he retrieved it. This time he dove after it but the ruck was still able to roll part way down. Good comedy relief. Ended up being ambushed there. Got our stuff blown away.

SLEEP: none                          TOTAL: 0 Hours
                                     Missed Meals: L


## 27 JUNE 1980 (Mountain Phase: Day 25)

> My personal philosophy is that the best outfits are those wherein a procedure is developed whereby every man who has an idea on a particular subject may bring it forward at the time of discussion, without the slightest criticism or hesitation. He argues for his point of view *when you're discussing* exactly how you're going to proceed. ... Once the decision is *made*, however, 'This is the way we're going to do it,' bang, everybody complies. If a man doesn't comply, his official head should roll.
>
> General Curtis Le May,
> MISSION WITH LE MAY, 1965

The route back to the friendly forward unit was easy; all down hill along a trail. Good. Ended up having the damn M60 for 22 hours. I walked over more trees than I walked around. The squad calls me Tarzan—all brawn, no brains?

We returned to Camp Merrill by 0645. We turned in our special equipment, debriefed, and showered. Felt great. Still hungry after lunch. Nothing planned for the afternoon. An easy and hot 94-degree day. Picked up some items at the local PX for the squad.

Pigged out at dinner with two complete meals. I was so full I couldn't even go to church. Bad decision. They had donuts, soda, and pretty girls. Oh well, a hazard of war.

Packed up and prepared for the lower mountains. Only 45 percent of the company passed their patrols. A very low percentage mostly because of lack of cooperation.

SLEEP: 272300—280400                    TOTAL: 5 Hours
                                        Missed Meals: none


## 28 JUNE 1980 (Mountain Phase: Day 26)

> In regard to mountain warfare in general, everything de-
> pends on the skill of our subordinate officers and still more
> on the morale of our soldiers. Here it is not a question of
> skillful maneuvering, but of warlike spirit and wholehearted
> devotion to the cause.
>
> Major General Carl von Clausewitz,
> PRINCIPLES OF WAR, 1812

The lower mountains. The area was only a mile or so away so we took a little jaunt through the woods at 0630. The company was divided into three groups. We rotated through stations dealing with knots, rappelling, and rope bridge building. We did three types of rappelling: left and right handed rappelling off the 30-foot wood slat tower, full combat equipment rappelling, and the Australian frontal rappelling where you run forward, straight down the wall. What a blast. One's fears disappear after the first five feet of any of these rappels.

Spent about seven hours on knots today, going over twelve different types. A lot of time on our feet but most of it was stationary and in the shade. It was a good and easy day. There's even a beautiful waterfall here upon which you can rest your eyes when you get the opportunity, which, unfortunately, is not often.

During the afternoon, one group of Rangers held their class sitting waist deep in the creek.

SLEEP: 290100—290430                TOTAL: 3.5 Hours
                                     Missed Meals: none

## 29 JUNE 1980 (Mountain Phase: Day 27)

**With brave infantry and bold commanders, mountain ranges can usually be forced.**
Lieutenant General Antoine-Henri Baron de Jomini,
SUMMARY OF THE ART OF WAR, 1838

Now we're into the good stuff. Rappelling down the 60-foot cliff. We did two 'Hollywood'—no equipment—rappels, two with equipment, and two with bounds. We then did some special rappels—buddy and stretcher. A lot of fun except for the equipment rappels. It's significantly less entertaining for the one strapped into the stretcher, his life entrusted to other rookies.

Five Rangers almost bought the farm today, fatal hookups where the rope slides off the D-ring. This usually brought a response of "You daredevil, you!" from the RI in addition to some other highlighting verbiage.

One Ranger's rappel seat became undone while doing an equipment repel. He and a second Ranger turned completely upside down with their feet sticking straight up in the air with one of them screaming as he turned turtle. Another Ranger's M16 fell off at the cliff's edge. We were lucky it didn't hit anyone on the way down. It really proved not to be his day. He was also one with a fatal hookup. Rangers who fouled up badly did pushups in the creek.

The company is falling apart pretty badly now. We act as if it's all over. One Ranger's weapon was so badly rusted, the inspecting RI couldn't even move the selector switch off safe. The Tac NCO was livid and all hell broke loose. A real witch-hunt developed as the RIs inspected all of our weapons.

It rained for an hour or two this afternoon. First, the sky turned black. Then the wind picked up and the rain could be heard advancing through the woods towards us—a moving wall of water. It was an eerie thing to listen and watch. Our weapons are really beat up and, during an inspection after dinner, everyone was written up. Needless to say, we spent the evening cleaning them while practicing our knots. Turns out the Tacs had good things to say about our squad's hooch. Supposedly, it stood out. Not bad. A good ending to a tough day.

SLEEP: 300001—300430                         TOTAL: 4.5 Hours
                                             Missed Meals: none

## 30 JUNE 1980 (Mountain Phase: Day 28)

**When confronted with a situation, do not try to recall examples given in any particular book on the subject; do not try to remember what your instructor said ... do not try to carry in your minds patterns of particular exercises or battles, thinking they will fit new cases, because no two sets of circumstances are alike.**

General of the Armies John J. Pershing, 1918,
Address to the 1st Infantry Division,
BLACK JACK, 1977

Test day. During the morning, we practiced bounding from atop the 30-foot tower. Some Rangers finished their bounds hanging upside down, bouncing like a yo-yo, as they'd lose their balance with the last bound and get caught up in the rope. We also built a suspension traverse.

After lunch, we had a diagnostic test on knots. Our squad went to the rope corral first for the final test. We had to pass eight of twelve knots. If a Ranger maxed the test, he would receive a superior plus spot report. If 50 percent of our class maxed—fat chance of that happening, the company would have PX and phone privileges. Forget it. In my squad alone, there were three No Goes and no max's.

I failed one knot. The RI beat the tar out of my coiled bowline knot to loosen it a bit. "You are a No Go with this knot, Ranger!" We're lucky if 10 percent of the company maxed, let alone 50 percent.

Other tests included rappelling with equipment and belaying. Unfortunately, there were a lot of failures. Mac failed both the knots and belaying. It proved to be an all around bad day for him.

We arrived back at camp in time for dinner. Patrol leaders and assistant patrol leaders were assigned for our next day's mission. We started work on the Warning and Operations Order after dinner. The Warning Order was finished around 2130.

What a joke. We have an American 2LT who has selective difficulty reading and speaking English. He was clueless about orders—or anything else for that matter—so he attempted to deliver the Warning Order in pidgin English. He was relieved on the spot and given a No Go.

Of course, Lady Luck was smiling my way, for I was selected to assume the patrol leader duties. Great. I wish she'd leave me alone for awhile. The worst time to be in a leadership position—planning—for it is one that almost everyone fails.

It would not have been such a significant problem except for one factor: I knew nothing about the mission! I had not been to the patrol leader briefings earlier, nothing had been started planning wise, and here it was 2200 with taps at 2300. Oh well, no joy in Mudville tonight. It would just have to be one hell of a pullout.

I immediately organized things and got the squad off and running building a terrain model, drawing and checking equipment, writing annexes, and sketching charts. What is it that Scarlet says in *Gone With The Wind*, "Tomorrow's another day?" Well, I sure hope so.

SLEEP: 302330—010430                    TOTAL: 5 Hours
                                        Missed Meals: none

## 01 JULY 1980 (Mountain Phase: Day 29)

**[In reference to Mutiny] Where soldiers get into trouble of this nature, it is nearly always the fault of some officer who has failed his duty.**
Field Marshal Viscount Montgomery of Alamein,
PSYCHIATRY IN THE BRITISH ARMY IN WWII, 1958

All right. Worked out a new time schedule. It will be a tight fit for the Operations Order but we can handle it. I worked on coordinating fire support, routes, and organizing the order until the briefing at 0930. Everything went off practically as planned. I gave much of it off the cuff and straight out of the Ranger Handbook.

After finishing the Operations Order and conducting rehearsals, we went to the airfield for our airmobile insertion. There, the RI pulled me aside and said that I had done an excellent job—which translated to a Go. Then I was relieved. Yes! Can just cruise this mission—or so I hope.

The insertion took place 25 kilometers from camp, a round—about fifteen minute ride—for aviators never fly in a straight line, or 'as the crow flies', unless they have to. We flew past the Tennessee Valley Divide. A whole lot of BFRs down there. Once we landed, we had to gouge our way from the landing zone to the objective, and I do mean gouge. This is the worst underbrush we've hit yet. At least elsewhere, we could use trails. Here we can't. They're too large and open. I was point man and the thorns tore the hell out of me. I walked on a four foot black snake on the way to the objective rally point. I just love these snakes.

At the objective rally point, I took over the M60. It was a good deal for it gave me a break by ensuring I would not be part of the leader's recon. After the recon, we had a long haul up Tifton Mountain. The ravine we used was exceptionally steep. We proceeded to establish a patrol base near the top.

Everything fell apart from that moment on. The squad slept, ate, and basically did what it wanted. The patrol leader allowed it to continue and consequently was No Go'd. Not that he really cared, for he already had a Go in the mountains. The RI was pretty lenient. He did not write any major minus spot reports; just let us boil in our own stew so to say.

I heated some water for my Long Range Reconnaissance Patrol (LRRPs) meal—a special treat we rarely got. They are very similar to MREs but, for some reason, they always seem to taste so much better. Um ... um ... good. I suppose just about anything tastes great when you are hungry and have nothing else to look forward to.

Routinely, I save cocoa and coffee packets from my C-rats. They definitely come in handy. I have a running bet with a classmate. He believes that by the end of Ranger School, I will be dipping and chewing just like the rest, needing the nicotine to stay awake. No way. I may be a Ranger but I do have some minimum standards—placing that garbage in my mouth is too nasty a habit for me. Instead, I've opted for a caffeine high to keep me awake. The coffee and cocoa packets are reportedly double or triple the normal levels of caffeine. I combine the contents of these packets in a single plastic bag with the cream and sugar that also comes with the rations. The resulting mixture is not only more potent than tobacco, but it also psychologically falls within the category of food. While I admit it may be an acquired taste, it certainly serves its purpose. Chew on some of this witch's brew and you will not need a light to see at night—your eyes will open so wide their whites will serve as headlight beacons!

Nights in the mountains are pretty cool even in the midst of summer. There is a lot of wind on top of these hills. I was able to change my sweaty fatigues. What comfort.

SLEEP: 020100—020300                              TOTAL: 2 Hours

                                                         Missed Meals: L

## 02 JULY 1980 (Mountain Phase: Day 30)

**Tact: the ability to describe others as they see themselves.**
Abraham Lincoln

Peeked out from under my poncho liner at 0300 and prepared to depart the patrol base. At 0400, we went admin and the RI had me critique the patrol's performance from the time of the airmobile. Recalling the necessity for tact from my peer rating experience, my autopsy on our activities to date proved to be both professional—at least according to the RI—and non combative—a key objective of mine. Who knows. Maybe an old dog can learn knew tricks.

We departed the patrol base and proceeded over the top of the mountain. In the process, I lost my black gloves. The mountain giveth and the mountain taketh away. We went down the other side, overshot our turnoff, and had to reclimb part of the mountain. Having to do this while lugging the M60 did not make for a pleasant experience. We finally hit the trail that ran all the way to our pickup zone, a little over four clicks. Oh, my doubly aching feet. Fortunately, we did not have to gouge our way there.

The choppers picked us up and provided a great fifteen-minute ride at 130 mph. As the first man in the door, the wind buffeted my legs as we sat on the floorboards. We touched down at the camp, dropped off our equipment, cleaned our weapons, and showered. No lunch. Damn.

The company had a 75 percent pass rate this time on patrols. That meant PX privileges. We could buy $1 worth of pogie bait. Of course, I bought $2.50 worth. The down side to this was that I had only ten minutes to eat it all because our platoon was the last to enter the PX and there was to be a company formation at 1705. Not a great idea on a stomach not used to this stuff. I lost count but I believe the final total was 50 cookies in ten minutes.

Ended up pretty bloated after supper. It's only the second time since I've been in the course that I've had that feeling. Brought some pogie back to the hooch even though it was unauthorized. I sure as hell was not going to throw it out.

We all went to sleep early. I had guard from 0100–0200. Employing various techniques learned here at Ranger school, a buddy and I were able to infiltrate the occupied fire station, purchase some sodas from a machine, and extract ourselves undetected. What a great coup. It's pretty depressing to realize that we've been reduced to this for excitement.

We hit the upper mountain tomorrow. Bad news, another of my Ranger buddies failed his patrol for being lost.

SLEEP: 022100—030400                    TOTAL: 6 Hours
(minus 1 hr for guard)                  Missed Meals: B L

## 03 JULY 1980 (Mountain Phase: Day 31)

**Darkness is a friend to the skilled infantryman.**
Captain Sir Basil Liddell Hart,
THOUGHTS ON WAR, 1944

Up at 0400. After a quick breakfast, we were trucked by 5 tons to mount Yonah. The ride took thirty to forty minutes. We detrucked on the highway and marched a few miles with rucks to the site.

We spent the entire afternoon doing 50-foot bounding rappels, free climbs, and buddy climbs. I burnt the hell out of my hand on a 50-foot bound. It was an excellent bound with a big push-off and fast drop. I tried to slow my decent with my brake hand but inadvertently—or should I say naturally—clamped my guide hand, also. The result was two big blisters. I hit the ground with my feet well planted. Unfortunately, the velocity of my drop was a bit more than I had anticipated. The force of the hit drove me into a deep squat that nearly caused me to bruise the ol' tail bone. On the free climb, I had to do pushups, a normal routine for me, facing down the mountain.

Before supper, we put up a bivouac site. After dinner, we held skits, sang, and danced if you can believe that. The Zairians always lead a crazy chant. Pretty neat.

One RI planned to make another RI the butt of his joke. It did not take much to enlist me and another student in the effort. The two RIs ended up challenging each other to a strength competition. After a bit of toying around, the target RI was convinced to lie on the ground to try and lift two big men lying next to him. Once the second Ranger student and I were next to the RI, we interlocked our arms and legs. Upon realizing that he had been 'had,' the RI attempted to extract himself from the ambush, but to no avail. He wasn't going anywhere. He couldn't budge an inch.

Armed with a full can of shaving cream, the other RI made short work of his buddy. He was plastered from head to foot. What a nice feeling of satisfaction, a sense of accomplishment.

At 2100, we went to the top of Yonah. It was very peaceful, even calming, with a great breeze. I didn't want to come down. Our rappel that evening was a 200-foot drop into pitch black. You couldn't tell where the bottom of the cliff was in the tree line. My lane was steep but it proved to be a good rappel.

As it so happened, the most dangerous part of the evening was the walk back to our bivouac site as we stumbled along in the dark.

SLEEP: 040030–040430                    TOTAL: 4 Hours
                                        Missed Meals: none


## 04 JULY 1980 (Mountain Phase: Day 32)

> Those who wage war in mountains should never pass through defiles without first making themselves masters of the heights.
>
> Field Marshal Maurice Comte de Saxe,
> MY REVERIES, 1732

Happy holiday. Celebrate your independence. We devoted this morning to advanced buddy and tension climbs. The buddy climb was not too bad; only one shaky portion.

The tension climb was an altogether different animal. Approximately 50 feet up the cliff, it turned out that the previous climber in front of me had taken, not one, but two snap link D-rings from the anchoring pitons. The two most crucial ones for, without them, I was literally left hanging under a ledge. I had to wait 15 additional minutes while an RI lowered two replacement snap links down to me. Putting them back in place was one of the greatest strains I have ever undergone. I must confess that I leveled more than a few select curses and threats to the individual responsible as I worked to replace the links, much to the amusement of everyone—which probably included the culprit, himself.

Later, my Ranger Buddy had to clear the tension climb lane of snap links. Moving up the cliff, he took full advantage of my belay position by falling at every opportunity. He almost cut me in half a couple of times with his falls. For all intent and purposes, I pulled him up that damn mountain. Hell of a work out. Some other Rangers had nasty falls of over 15 feet, even with safety lines tied around them.

We finished around 1300 and walked down the side of the mountain to the trucks. The weather's been draining: 95 degrees, high humidity for a week.

We arrived back at camp, drew weapons, showered, and ate. Because of the holiday, the RIs are taking a break. They will not issue the mission statement at 1530, as usual, for the start of our five-day patrol. Instead, they're waiting until tomorrow morning.

SLEEP: 042230—050330         TOTAL: 5 Hours

Missed Meals: none

## 05 JULY 1980 (Mountain Phase: Day 33)

**In battles and in every action against the enemy the wise general, even the most courageous, will keep in mind the possibility of failure and defeat and will plan for them as actually occurring.**

The Emperor Mauice,
THE STRATEGIKON, AD 600

Day one of our five-day patrol. Up at 0330. The mission will be given at 0400. Our platoon ate last this morning. We ended up with a grand total of five minutes to eat breakfast. Damn, still rushing these meals.

The patrol Operations Order went at 1000. There was very little time to complete everything. We airmobiled at 1400. Proved to be a good insertion. As primary compass man, I led the way to the objective. On target. Terrain mostly ridges and fingers along the way. Arrived at the objective rally point (ORP) at 1500.

The new mission called for an ambush at 2215. We set up surveillance of the ambush site and hunkered down for some sleep. The ambush went off at the correct time, but the patrol leader botched it by hesitating and not assaulting through the objective in a timely manner. The enemy reacted well, forcing us to withdrawal into the wood line and race—if you can call limping about on abused legs racing— up a hill. Boy, now wasn't that fun. We got our asses kicked on that one. Finally, we stopped, took accountability, and critiqued the actions.

We moved out at 0001. At the bottom of the hill, our headcount showed one missing. After a roll call, it turned out we were short one cadet. The RI went on a tear after the Ranger's hide and found him sleeping back at the rally point (RP).

Once our missing sheep was returned to the fold, we took to the road to cross a bridge. There were plenty of campers about—4th of July weekend, national park, civilization. We trudged by in the dark. We could see them around their campfires but they could not see us in the dark. All they could do was gaze into the blackness and wonder what the clinking of equipment and shuffling of feet were all about. It must have been a pretty eerie feeling for some of them thinking "Big Foot" was roaming about. Felt pretty bad for us, too, watching them. All I could think was how lucky those SOBs were.

SLEEP: 051930—052200         TOTAL: 2.5 Hours
Missed Meals: L D

## 06 JULY 1980 (Mountain Phase: Day 34)

> To seduce the enemy's soldiers from their allegiance and encourage them to surrender is of especial service, for an adversary is more hurt by desertion than by slaughter.
> Flavius Vegetius Renatus
> THE MILITARY INSTITUTIONS OF THE ROMANS,
> c. AD 378

After we left the vicinity of the campsites, the RI tried to take us off road and have us travel through a clear cut area—fields where trees have been cut down and left—to our patrol base. That attempt proved to be a non-starter from the moment the idea was conceived. It was pitch black and we couldn't see squat. I was still point man and, as I fell forward over one tree in particular, I grabbed hold of a thick stick as I hit the ground. Unfortunately, the "stick" decided to slither out of my hand. I must admit this great Ranger warrior let out one hell of a scream as I staggered to my feet cursing about the lineage of snakes dating back to the Garden of Eden. We traveled 25 meters before the RI admitted defeat, called a retreat, and conducted a retrograde operation back to the road. Personally, I don't believe everyone left the road in the first place—they were no fools.

We ended up taking the road all the way to our patrol base. If we hadn't done that, we'd have been out there for days. No trouble staying awake tonight for me, though many others are walking dead. The RI gave out a number of Goes before he left and plus spot reports to those who did special jobs. I was a fortunate recipient of one of those spot reports but, unfortunately, that only makes up for one third of the major minus I will probably receive for not coughing tactically last night—noise discipline, you know. Just can't win.

We stayed at the patrol base until 1700. We departed on a mission but no one knew what was going on. I have the M60 once again—my buddy. We humped over ridges, along some trails, and gouged our way to the objective rally point—a long haul. The weather's hot and humid. The only relief is along the ridge lines where there is normally a breeze. Ridgelines are also great sites to be ambushed, and we were.

At the objective, I was on the right flank support. The "commie pinkos" on the objective were yelling and taunting the "American swine" they knew to be out and about soliciting our surrender. Drunk civilians from the July 4th weekend were parked and watching from their cars and the wood lines. I wonder what they think of this show? Finally, opened up and put 200 rounds (of blanks) on the objective. I ended up burning the hell out of my arm reaching for the sling over a very hot M60 barrel. Slick move, Lock.

Moved up to the objective rally point in the dark, picked up our rucks, and humped along a trail over the top of the hill. No moon. We walked right into another ambush. We're beyond the point of caring. We just walked through it like zombies, all 35 of us—two sections that linked up as a platoon the first morning of the mission.

We finally had to leave the trail and gouge a path. It was a long haul, especially with the M60. I crashed and burned twice. The first time I have actually hit the ground. I almost fractured my knees falling on some large rocks. My second drop had me falling over backwards, into a gully. I came up and out of the entanglement as mad as a bear.

We finally reached the patrol base but what a cluster along the way. The RIs moved us to a better location. There, we became a clandestine patrol base even though we were larger than a squad. It was a good night's rest even though it grew pretty chilly.

SLEEP: 070200—070530                    TOTAL: 3.5 Hours
                                        Missed Meals: L D

## 07 JULY 1980 (Mountain Phase: Day 35)

**Communications dominate war; broadly considered, they are the most important single element in strategy, political or military.**

> Rear Admiral Alfred Thayer Mahan,
> THE PROBLEM OF ASIA, 1900

Only two nights left out here. New RIs on hand. The last ones turned out all right despite first impressions. They gave almost everyone Goes.

Our Marine recycle just upped and quit this morning. He walked off with the relieved RIs. Seems he's had enough of this fun.

I am now the primary Radio Telephone Operator (RTO) for the next 24 hours just having come off being the M60 gunner for the past 24 hours. Oh my flat, aching feet. I gathered up the codes, call signs, and frequencies. I have to submit a Situation Report (SITREP) every hour. It keeps me busy, awake, and, in all honesty, it's enjoyable.

The only problem is lugging that PRC77 radio and accessories, an extra 25 to 30 pounds of equipment, on my back.

The patrol is going fast. One C-rat per Ranger and some ammo were air dropped from choppers today. Our drinking water is coming from the local creeks. At least it is fresh and appears to be clean. I hope those iodine tablets do their work. Looking forward to our Super Supper and break after the completion of this phase.

We prepared to depart the patrol base at 1600. The RIs talked to us for about an hour on tactics. We finally departed on a trail at 1700. The last part of the movement was gouging up, down, and around some mountains. What luck being the primary RTO carrying the PRC77, extra batteries, accessories, 320 rounds for the M60, an extra pair of boots, and clothes. Must be at least 70 pounds, which, by itself, is not much unless you have to hump it for 10 clicks. Then it begins to wear on you.

Hit the objective, after which, we staggered up hill to withdrawal. It should be 'downhill' to the patrol base from here by trail.

SLEEP: none                                     TOTAL: 0 Hours
                                              Missed Meals: L D

## 08 JULY 1980 (Mountain Phase: Day 36)

> **Soldiers must be taught to move and fight at night. This is becoming more and more imperative, and it does not mean to make an approach march at night. It means to conduct lethal operations in the dark. To do this, previous and very accurate daylight reconnaissance is desirable and limited objective attacks are essential.**
>
> General George S. Patton, Jr.,
> WAR AS I KNEW IT

WRONG! What hell ... what terror! It was a pitch black night and the patrol leader and compass man were having some serious operator 'head space and timing' problems. Yes, Les, ol' buddy, this is YOUR story.

We never did hit that trail we were looking for after the raid. Instead, we hit contours, ravines, creeks, marshes, and cliffs. I fell twice with the PRC77—once into a creek as I was crossing over a log when I forgot about the law of nature referred to as center of gravity.

The other fall occurred when I took a step and found only air for a free fall of about six feet. This fall was the result of an interesting phenomena. While trudging along in the night in a Ranger file, one maintains contact with the Ranger in front by focusing on the cat eyes sewn onto the back of his PC—in addition to the luminous dial of the lensatic compass thrown over his shoulder. The problem is that the luminous image, over time, eventually is indelibly etched onto the retina of your eyes. Consequently, when it disappears, as it did when the Ranger in front of me walked off the same cliff, you still "see" those cat eyes before you. I would have fractured my knee caps on a large slab of rock if it hadn't been for the gaggle of struggling Rangers already on the ground below who broke my fall.

We ended up walking four hours straight, 0001–0400, everywhere imaginable, and a few unimaginable, looking for this damn trail that we crossed in the dark at least three times. Of course, whenever we crossed the trail we opted not to take it. We just kept walking to the top of every mountain we were on.

Finally, after one of our halts near the top of a mountain, I fought my way up a ravine to find out what the hell was going on. At the top, I found Les, the patrol leader, and the compass man huddled under a poncho liner looking at their maps with a red lens flashlight. Periodically, Les would peer out from under the poncho, gaze about—what he was looking at I couldn't guess because it was so damn dark—and then zip back under the poncho liner like a scavenger scurrying back into its hole with some new little morsel of information to consume. Finally, Les turned off the light, threw the poncho to the ground, looked about at us, and stated with no undo conviction, "Yep, that's it." A flicker of hope? Unfortunately, with the wave of a hand, he pointed off in the distance and continued with, "The mountain top we want is over there!" Shit! Lord help me. This really does suck. I love you Les, old buddy, old pal, but it was miserable.

Immediately saddling up, we began our movement down the mountain. What fun. We took a ravine all the way. It made for a quick journey down but, because of the steepness, we were literally sliding on our butts the whole way.

At the bottom, we had another of our numerous creek crossings. This one, though, proved to be a bit different for we came upon a huge, and I do mean huge, tree that was lying on its side on the far bank. It was so dark—how dark was it you ask? It was so dark that you needed a second match to see if your first match was lit; you could not even see the tree if you stood with your nose touching its bark.

In retrospect, we must have looked like the three blind men examining an elephant with each man identifying the object as something different. Why we elected to go over rather than around this object, I'll never know. Personal pride? Because we're Rangers? No … I'd say it was because we were stupid. Brute force and ignorance seems to be our motto at times.

In order to get over this "Redwood," one had to sit straddled on the tree and pull another up as a third pushed from below. I wonder how the last Ranger got up the tree? Probably walked around it—the only smart one in the group. I only wish I knew what the RI thought of this whole episode.

On the other side of the tree, we found an incline that was at least 60 percent. After initially trying to walk up it by grabbing small trees, we finally had to drop to our knees and crawl for approximately 100 meters. We hit a road that provided us with a short breather.

Unfortunately, the hill increased in slope on the other side—the road was really a cut in the side of the mountain. We ended up climbing on our hands and knees for another 100 meters or so. Finally, we hit our patrol base site.

What a terrible, miserable night—sweaty, chilly, and no sleep because as primary RTO, I had to make a hourly Situation Report. What a grind. At least I have the PRC77, CEOI, KAL61B (encryption codes), and Tac Ops down.

RIs changed. How you got a Go, Les, I'll never know but congrats. Must have been that drive-on despite the adversity leadership!

I was initially named as the patrol leader. No sleep, no food, no anything but misery for the rest of the day. No way. Fortunately, it turned out to be a mistake. Others needed Goes, not I. My consolation prize was to be made a squad leader. That's almost as bad, damn it. Contrary to my initial expectations, though, it turned out for the better. The RI taught me a lot about being a squad leader. The experience turned out to be a good one, I had to admit, and somehow, I even managed to squeeze in eating my last two C-rats.

We were ambushed in the patrol base around 1600. Artillery simulators were thrown right on top of some of the Rangers. Fortunately, no one was hurt and the attack was stopped. The RIs did not require us to leave the patrol base as normal tactics would dictate.

We departed the patrol base at 1700 after a good hour-long talk led by the RIs. Not much trouble moving to the objective. Mostly trails with little gouging. Good RIs who gave us pointers on land nav techniques. At the objective rally point, I was placed in charge of the support element. Set up the M60s—two with me on the right flank at a bend in the road. At 2200, four vehicles, two of them 5-ton cargo trucks with mounted M60s, moved into our ambush. Our guns lit them up with four minutes of continuous fire. The assault line moved forward across the objective.

Surprise! Another convoy. This one also had four vehicles, three of which were 5 tons with mounted M60s. They fired up our assault line but made one significant mistake. They stopped right in front of my support position approximately 10 feet away. Blew them away ... total and complete annihilation—or so it would have been if it were real. Great fun. Our assault line finished their mission, blew some quarter sticks of TNT, and withdrew.

Admin time. The ambushed convoys moved out followed by a bunch of civilians in cars—about ten of them—who stopped to watch the festivities or collect the spent brass blank ammunition casings for future sale as scrap metal. It was pretty funny. I really do wonder what they think. Finally, we moved out for the patrol base.

SLEEP: none                                    TOTAL: 0 Hours
                                               Missed Meals: L

## 09 JULY 1980 (Mountain Phase: Day 37)

**No human being knows how sweet sleep is but a soldier.**
Colonel John S. Mosby,
MOSBY'S WAR REMINISCENCES

Compass/point man to the patrol base. Seems they just will not leave me alone with these jobs—persecution complex? We started off by taking a trail around 0030. After 100 meters, we moved into a clear cut. Crash and burn city. One Ranger, a former Ranger Buddy of mine, kept going to the right, downhill, while I was moving with the patrol to the left. The end result was that he kept falling into the creek and thrashing about. I'd pick him out of the creek, we'd walk a little farther, he'd fall into the creek, and I'd pull him out again—his internal "which way is up" stabilizing adjusters must have been down or they were in serious need of recalibration. Couldn't help but laugh out loud. We headed up a hill and hit the trail again.

Once on the trail, we moved pretty quickly through some camp grounds. The RIs tried to smoke us on this movement, but no way. They ended up being extremely impressed with our enthusiasm for the fifth day of this patrol. We stopped short of the patrol base to establish it. I went along on the leader's recon of the site and was left behind as security while the PL went back for the others.

What did I then do? I fell asleep! This was only the second time I've done that. I must admit I was at the far end of my power curve. When did I last sleep? It seems to be days. The next thing I heard was the following sweet nothing whispered so tenderly and lovingly into my ear: "Ranger, are you asleep?" Of course, I answered as any good Ranger would with a loud and resounding "No, RI!" Still somewhat in a daze—the fog of war, I saw the RI flash a light on the weapon I was carrying, an M14, and order me to pull the trigger. In my semiconscious state, I almost did. Turns out the RI had taken the weapon off safe and placed it on automatic. That definitely would have cleared a few cobwebs. Minus spot report. Oh hell ... like I needed another.

The patrol slept from 0400 to 0530. I was too keyed up after my run-in with the RI to do so. Turns out our patrol finished earlier than the others. The RI took us to a parking lot where we waited a hour for the other patrols to finish.

The truck ride back to camp took nearly one-and-a-half hours. Good, if not comfortable, rack time. Back at camp, we dropped off our equipment, turned in weapons, cleaned up, got haircuts—certainly a top Ranger priority—and ran details. Our Super Supper was not so good, but it didn't make much difference for it seems our stomachs have shrunk and most of us did not eat much, anyway.

That night, we were able to go to the NCO club. Mac and I had some beer—sooooo good—and food. We ended up staying after closing, 2300, to assist with the clean up, though, I will admit, we had ulterior motives. The bartenders were RIs who kept placing free pitchers of beer before us—our ulterior motive—as we cleaned. Ultimately, all of us were drunk. Finally, at 0001, we hit the rack after 2 to 3 pitchers apiece.

SLEEP: 090001—090200               TOTAL: 2 Hours
                                   Missed Meals: B

## 10 JULY 1980 (Mountain Phase: Day 38)

> Our military forces are one team—in the game to win regardless of who carries the ball. This is no time for 'fancydans' who won't hit the line with all they have on every play, unless they can call the signals. Each player on the team—whether he shines in the spotlight of the backfield or eats dirt in the line—must be All-American.
>
> General of the Army Omar N. Bradley,
> 19 October 1949, testimony in Congress

In bed at 0001. I was supposed to have guard at 0200. I volunteered even though I am now a platoon sergeant in the chain of command. Lead by example, right? The Field Marshall apparently tried to wake me up. Says he did everything short of detonating a tactical nuclear weapon under my bunk. He went on guard for a few minutes to cover for me and then came back to try again. When he returned the second time, he found me up, leaning against the wall sleeping, like a horse. He should have left me there but, instead maneuvered me back to the bunk. I never did stand guard that night.

The company was roused shortly thereafter around 0230, ate a quick breakfast and then loaded on the buses, Fort Benning bound, for the four hour return trip. Pulled into Benning in time to witness the class ahead of us graduating. Almost there. One more phase to go. Did what we had to do which included appointing a new chain of command. Yeah. My additional duty as a platoon sergeant had come to a close.

We also had our weight checked prior to going on break. It is periodically monitored to ensure we do not become cadavers. The RIs are stunned. While everyone else is running 10 to 15 pounds under their reporting weight, I am two pounds over at 198.

What's the secret? Milk, my boy, milk. In garrison, we can drink all we want at the mess hall. I drink as much whole milk as my stomach will allow me to retain at each meal, which usually leaves my stomach somewhat extended and pregnant looking. The strategy seems to have worked so far, though I certainly did not tell the RIs this. If I did, they'd probably cut off my source and recycle me for not undergoing the full Ranger experience.

Yesterday during counseling, I found out that I did get a major minus spot report for not coughing tactfully. There was some good news, though. Apparently, the other RI let me off in reference to the major minus for sleeping, and I received a minor plus for compass and RTO duties. The chain of command also got plus spots for good work. Seems they gave me a major plus for my platoon sergeant duties. Eventually, I suppose, everything begins to even out. Isn't that supposed to be the natural course of events? I'm finally out of the hole and at the break even point in reference to spot reports. About time. It's a real pain being borderline all the time as I have been.

On our break by 1500. Pigged out, especially on pizza, and washed our clothes at a laundromat. There was not enough time to drop them off for someone else to do. Four of us roamed about terrorizing the countryside in a van. The temperature the last few days has been in the 100s. Hot and humid. Ah ...

We finished our break at 2100. It was over much too quickly. Another cluster in prepping for the next phase: organizing equipment, packing, etc. In bed by 2230.

And by the way, that slug of a captain I noted on Day 21 was peered again and tossed from the course. No great loss, there. He never attempted to be a team player and, consequently, paid the price. His loss, not ours.

SLEEP: 102230—110300                              TOTAL: 4.5 Hours
                                                 Missed Meals: none

*****

## *TWO PHASES DOWN: ONE TO GO*

*****

# MOUNTAIN PHASE

*Welcome to our new home at Camp Merrill. Decades worth of Ranger classes passed through these hooches with many of them leaving words of wisdom etched on the inner walls for generations of Rangers yet to pass.*

*Planning Bay #20. Many a plan came together here, some good, some not so good.*

*Lower mountaineering. This site could have proven to be the last for a few of our classmates who had fatal hookups. "You Daredevil, you!"*

*It wasn't the rappelling, alone, that was dangerous. Just getting out to the rappel rope was a challenge in and of itself.*

*A buddy rappel. Not my idea of fun, especially if I were the one riding on someone's back…like the "Field Marshal" here.*

*Wherever we traveled in the mountain phase, our Swiss seats, D-rings, and gloves were always by our sides.*

*Yohna Mountain off in the distance—our upper mountain training site.*

*Choppers touching down as we prepare to be lifted from a PZ ... pickup zone.*

*Insertion at the LZ ... landing zone. Security established. The scene of many an ambush.*

# CHAPTER 7

# RANGER SCHOOL: FLORIDA PHASE

We should choose the terrain not only to suit our armament, but also with a view to the various peoples. Parthians and Gauls handle themselves well on the Plains. The Spanish and Ligurians fight better in the mountains and hills, and the Britons in the woods, while the Germans are more at home in the swamps. Whatever terrain the general chooses, he should make his troops familiar with it. They will then be able to avoid the rough spots and because of their knowledge of the area will fight the enemy with confidence.

The Emperor Maurice,
THE STRATEGIKON, c. AD600

The third and final phase of Ranger School is conducted at Camp James E. Rudder...Auxiliary Field #6...at Eglin Air Force Base, Florida, by the 6th Ranger Training Battalion. Considered the most extreme in terms of physical and mental stress, Camp Rudder exposes the Ranger students to the harsh and oppressive environment of the Florida jungle and swamp where they will learn boat drills, make one-rope bridges, and negotiate rivers and swamps. This final phase is the toughest and most demanding. Exhausted and emaciated, only the toughest and most dedicated Rangers usually see it through to the end.

The first day of the phase begins with outdoor classes to review patrol base operations, duties and responsibilities of platoon leaders and platoon sergeants, and the mechanics of zone reconnaissance. The Ranger cadre review and demonstrate ambush and raid techniques prior to introducing the students to movement-to-contact tactics. This day is closed out with a live demonstration of snakes and alligators and a discussion of how to identify and avoid the reptiles. For those who may fail to avoid them, we were also trained on how to treat snakebites.

The second and third days are spent in the field. Attrited to platoon size, the companies spend the two nights in a patrol base while practicing their ambushes, raids, and movement to contacts during the day.

On the fourth day, the training moves to the water environment where the students train on stream crossings and small-boat operations. All initial water operations begin with land training to get the sequence and timing down. Once the RIs feel the unit is competent enough, squad sized elements load aboard Zodiac boats and, accompanied by RIs, paddle to a patrol base in the swamp where they will spend the night.

Commencing that evening with the issuance of an Operations Order, the nine-day field exercise in the swamp begins. Crossing rivers with rope bridges, paddling up and down the rivers in their Zodiacs, or riding about in helicopters and C130s, the Ranger students will conduct reconnaissance, ambush, raid, airborne, and air assault missions.

The field training exercise and the Ranger course itself ends with a predawn amphibious assault across the Gulf of Mexico onto Santa Rosa Island. Beginning their assault preparations around 1600 hours, each company plans and rehearses for a coordinated attack. Embarking late that evening, the force hits the beach around 0400 where it is met by defenders who force the Ranger students to fight their way ashore.

Nearly sixteen days after arrival in Florida and having completed the amphibious assault and final after action review, the Ranger students are within days of receiving the Coveted Black and Gold. Clearing Camp Rudder and returning to Camp Rogers at Ft. Benning, the cycle is complete and graduation is in sight.

## 11 JULY 1980 (Florida Phase: Day 39)

**Where is the Prince who can afford so to cover this country with troops for its defense, as that 10,000 men descending from the clouds, might not, in many places, do an infinite deal of mischief before a force could be brought together to repel them?**

Benjamin Franklin, 1784

Up at 0300. Baggage taken care of, off to breakfast, then briefings. The RIs from Florida are here to fly or jump with us, depending whether we are airborne or not, into the Florida Ranger Camp at Eglin Air Force Base Auxiliary Field 6. Of course, they had to pull our chain a little for fun so we played run-in and run-out games into and out of the classroom, as well as "hit it" and "check can-of-peas" airborne exercises.

Our mission was to plan an operation to rescue an American ambassador held hostage. For the mission, we only ended up with two C130s to fly all of us in. Problem was we had three platoons, three planes worth of Rangers.

Turned out Mac was not able to jump in. He came down with an intestinal virus from drinking bad water on the last patrol. It hit him below the belt with a serious case of the 'runs.' The Field Marshall had it also; he drank from Mac's canteen. Their whole squad was treated for the virus this morning at the hospital...having missed their break...the worse kick of all. Missing the break, however, wasn't the worst of it as they realized the attending physician was about to recommend that they were all too ill to continue with the course. Violently disagreeing, they were able to wear the doctor down and convince him that he would not be accountable if they returned and failed to recover.

The C130s departed, one with airborne personnel who would jump in, the other, with nasty leg Rangers, would airland. Being a nasty leg, myself, I was with the third group who waited until 1600 for one of the C130s to return for us. The flight to Eglin was only 30 minutes but by then the mission was fragged for those on the ground to complete while we reported directly to the billets. What a shame—or should that read sham?

On the DZ, the Field Marshall waited, remaining awake by switching the PRC77 radio to the low end of the frequency band where he was able to listen to the television Channel 6 movie, "Kingdom of the Spiders." While it wasn't "Urban Cowboy," it was better than nothing.

Upon our arrival, we picked up some basic issue, received some briefings from the camp commander, and moved into the billets by 2030 hours. Nice billets: big, brick, and air conditioned—when they elect to turn it on, and large latrines with plenty of hot water. Definitely the best we've had as Rangers.

The bagged lunch, though, that we had for dinner, left much to be desired. Two scrawny pieces of chicken—definitely not Frank Perdue grade—and two plain slices of bread. Holy shit! There was a little more but nothing worth mentioning. At least I had my pogie: sugar wafer cookies, pretzels, and soft Mounds. Soft because chocolate and coconut have a tendency to melt in 100+ degree temperatures.

SLEEP: 112330—120330        TOTAL: 4 Hours
Missed Meals: L

## 12 JULY 1980 (Florida Phase: Day 40)

**Weather is not only to a great extent a controller of the condition of ground, but also of movement. It is scarcely necessary to point out the influence of heat and cold on the human body, or the effect of rain, fog, and frost on tactical**

and administrative mobility; but it is necessary to appreci-
ate the moral effect of weather and climate, for in the past,
stupendous mistakes have resulted through deficiency in
this appreciation.

Major General J.F.C. Fuller,
THE FOUNDATION OF THE SCIENCE OF WAR,
1926

Up early. Not a bad breakfast but the dining area is exceptionally warm.
We're sweating heavily and it's only 0400. We trucked to the Gulf coast
for RB15 training. Really beautiful. How I'd love to spend some time
at the beach—without being in fatigues, that is. Ended up with about
an hour of rack time in the truck during the movement.

At the beach, the MEDEVAC chopper was positioned nearby with
its crew sitting in beach chairs looking like something out of MASH:
bathing suits, suntan lotion, sun glasses, and boots.

A camera crew followed us all day filming. We took the RB15
boats out into the surf and spent part of the morning with capsize
drills—flipping them over time and time again, learning how to get in
and out while in the water. The Gulf is definitely salty.

Back on shore, I led an assault on our Tacs. We threw them in the
water to get them nice and wet. Then we buried them in the sand up to
their necks. We finished it off with a family portrait taken with the
camera that I have been surreptitiously using to record our activities.
Despite all the searches, they have yet to find it.

We trucked back to the billets through the local towns. Ugh. Babes,
in bikinis yet. Pure torture and no doubt intentional. Really not worth
thinking about, though. Even if we had the opportunity to mingle, it
would make no difference for we are an exceptionally sorry looking lot
by now.

We spent the afternoon building one-rope bridges and poncho
rafts. We were soaked all day and so was everything we placed in our
poncho rafts. Finished by 1800. Just in time for another of those
wonderful bagged lunches. This one was a wee bit better than our last
one.

It is extremely hot and muggy here. If we hadn't waded (waddled?) into the creek during our break this afternoon, there would undoubtedly have been a few heat casualties.

It's been 100+ degrees for quite a while now. Record breaking temperatures. Turns out this has been a killer heat wave this summer with over 250 people killed throughout the U.S. because of these extreme temperatures. Great time to be going through Ranger School. A temperature of 115 degrees is heat category one to them. No wet bulb here.

SLEEP: 122330—130430                    TOTAL: 5 Hours

                                        Missed Meals: none

## 13 JULY 1980 (Florida Phase: Day 41)

> Everybody gets frightened. This is basic. I do not believe that many soldiers are frightened of death. Most people are frightened of dying and everybody is frightened of being hurt. The pressures of noise, of weariness, of insecurity, lower the threshold of man's resistance to fear. All these sources of stress can be found in battle, and others too—hunger, thirst, pain, excess of heat or cold and so on. Fear in war finds victims fattened for the sacrifice.
>
> General Sir John Hackett,
> THE PROFESSION OF ARMS, 1983

Classes all morning today. The first one was on reptiles. 'Big John' is a 12.5-foot alligator weighing in at 755 pounds. Big, all right. They also showed us twelve different varieties of snakes. Some, the non-poisonous type, obviously, were passed around.

Then they brought out three others: a cottonmouth moccasin, diamondback rattlesnake and a king snake. The handler pretended to trip with one of them that caused a large group of reservists sitting in on the class with us to scatter in panic. We probably would have scattered also, but we were too tired to move in the face of potential death.

As for these snakes, damn, were they ever huge. The cottonmouth and diamondback were only four feet or so long but their bodies were as thick as my upper arm. Definitely cardiac arrest time if I run into one of these serpents in the field.

What's interesting is that while the king snake is nonpoisonous, it can supposedly take on any of the other two snakes and win. Maybe that's why the call it King? According to the RIs, they conducted a field experiment once to verify this. They placed an eight-foot rattler in a cage with a five-foot king snake. The rattler assumed an ostrich posture— as in burying its head under its body—immediately upon seeing the king snake. Two hours later, the rattler was dead. The king snake had asphyxiated it by constriction. Four hours later it had been completely consumed by the victor—though I am curious as to how an eight-foot snake can be consumed by a five-foot snake. Hell of an appetite. Maybe it's true and maybe it's not, but in either case stay away from me.

That afternoon we had classes on tracking. The RIs claim this is the only tracking course taught in the U.S. Army. During our practical exercise, another Ranger and I acted as prey. We left a 'natural' trail that anyone could follow—the pogie had to come out some time. It consisted of organic land mines with telltale white fuses—as in toilet paper. We've even learned how to urinate on the move for you do not have an opportunity to stop in the midst of a long movement to answer nature's call. My, what social skills we've mastered.

At 2100, we ran an escape and evasion course. We had three hours to move across country and link-up with a 'partisan' band. The company was organized into two and three man teams. I found myself part of a two-man team. Immediately after crossing the line of departure, my team linked up with another three Ranger team and waited. There is a mixture of thrill and trepidation of the unknown as one peers into the dark of the jungle. There were 'boo-coo' aggressors out there. We let other teams of Rangers try to get through first. Many of them were hunted down and captured quickly.

After a wait of thirty or so minutes, we moved out to the rally point, seven clicks away. Some things never change, for I was breaking brush the same way I did in the mountains—face first. I would have lost my eyes if it weren't for my glasses. How people without glasses make it through a night movement without having their eyes punctured, I'll never know.

The deadline for mission completion was 2400. Out of a feeling of futility, we almost stopped at 2355 but elected to drive on the last few minutes. One hundred meters later, we linked up with the friendly partisans. Mission accomplished.

We were able to sleep there from 0001 to 0330, though we were almost run over by a jeep a few minutes into our slumber as it came roaring down the trail to our location. Hindsight would indicate that our sleeping on the trail was not a smart idea. Only fourteen Rangers in the company completed the course successfully. The rest were captured and made to low crawl for hours as prisoners, or they were lost and had to be rounded up.

Turns out three Rangers—cadets—returned to the billets on their own. Since the company couldn't depart the area until everyone was accounted for, we didn't return to the billets until after 0400 when they were located. Their actions did not make us happy campers.

SLEEP: 140001—140330                    TOTAL: 4 Hours
       140430—140500                    Missed Meals: none

## 14 JULY 1980 (Florida Phase: Day 42)

> **Mistakes made in ordinary affairs can generally be remedied in a short while, but errors made in war cause lasting harm.**
> The Emperor Maurice,
> THE STRATEGIKON, c. AD600

Today, we had a cadre-led patrol to show us the ropes. Excellent RIs. Colonel Grange and Colonel Dewey Cameron came around and observed our training. Went over various aspects of patrolling in the jungle.

We had a block of instruction on patrolling with RB15s down the river. Our squad stinks on water. We snagged a submerged tree that resulted in a punctured and half-sunk boat. What a trip. Temperature today was up around 111 degrees, consequently, we were hopping in and out of the river to cool off between classes.

Conducted a one-rope bridge river crossing in an exceptionally muddy river. The swamp surrounding it was dry as a bone. Unfortunately, that left only us to occupy the horse flies, gnats, and mosquitoes. Another Ranger and I served as the right flank security during the river crossing operation. The only way to defeat the damn bugs was to cover up all exposed skin to include placing clothes over our heads. Great security—we couldn't see a thing.

It also turned out that the patrol leader had overlooked one minor attention-to-detail factor. He forgot to recall his right flank security— not that we were paying any particular attention ourselves, mind you. By the time we realized that we had been left behind, the patrol was on the other side of the river and the rope bridge was down. The RI was not amused. Rather than wait for them to put up the bridge, again, the other Ranger and I decided to combat swim across with LCE, ruck, and weapon. The river was thirty feet wide and ten feet deep. It was a cool swim—literally and figuratively—and we even managed to keep our weapons dry.

Training was canceled because of the heat after this. A first. We went over our brief-backs in the billets. The air-conditioning felt great as did the dry and clean set of fatigues I had an opportunity to change into. Finished our brief-backs by 1700. The temperature peaked at 112 degrees in the shade.

SLEEP: 142130—0430                    TOTAL: 7 Hours
                                      Missed Meals: none

## 15 JULY 1980 (Florida Phase: Day 43)

> Far from being a handicap to command, compassion is the
> measure of it. For unless one values the lives of his soldiers
> and is tormented by their ordeals, he is unfit to command.
> He is unfit to appraise the cost of an objective in terms of
> human lives. To spend lives, knowingly, deliberately—
> even cruelly—he must steel his mind with the knowledge
> that to do less would cost only more in the end. For if he
> becomes tormented by the casualties he must endure, he is
> in danger of losing sight of his strategic objectives. Where
> the objective is lost, the war is prolonged and the cost
> becomes infinitely worse.
>
> General of the Army Omar Bradley,
> A SOLDIER'S STORY

A very easy day. Classes in the morning on close air support (CAS). We saw some short flicks on the A-10 Warthog—complete with its 30mm tank busting cannon, the Specter Gunship, and Combat Talon C130. Not a bad time, especially since the room was air-conditioned.

After lunch, we practiced rappelling from the 30-foot tower. I was the third Ranger off the tower. My Ranger buddy was hurting so I agreed to rappel with his ruck. What a mistake. He had the PRC77 in his pack and to top it off, he had everything in it we were supposed to carry to include what felt like a brick or two. In exchange, he was able to rappel with my 'nerf' ruck that came in at approximately five pounds dripping wet.

Off the tower I went with this monster ruck. Burnt the hell out of my hands again—you'd think I'd learn by now how to brake properly—attaining maximum terminal velocity. I hit the ground in a deep squat, bouncing my butt off the compact dirt, and immediately executed a double somersault with full twist. Judge's score: 9.5. It took a while for the RIs to regain their composure and their breaths as I hung there upside down on the rope, bouncing my head off the ground. Personally, I failed to see the humor.

Unfortunately, the training was for naught; no choppers from Fort Rucker so we were unable to do any rappelling from live birds.

Well ... the temp is definitely creeping up there—118 degrees today. PX privileges at 1500. Pogie. The RIs must be getting soft in their old age. Another heat casualty. While sitting on our rucks, the Ranger just went catatonic. Not our normal catatonic state, mind you. He was pink, clammy, no sweat. All the classic symptoms. We dragged him off to the medic station. He was back to us within 24 hours, after they pumped him full of IV fluid.

Injuries are the greatest fear. You can only miss a total of 72 hours of training over the length of the course. If you miss more you will be recycled. Apparently the RIs have problems with Rangers becoming 'injured' on the last couple days of the Florida patrol. If they are 'Tabbed out' and have the 'sick leave' accumulated, some Rangers take the easy way out, leaving everyone else to suck it down.

After dinner, there was a quick downpour for all of five minutes. It was over before it began. The Ranger camp Tac NCO gave us another pep talk about cooperate and graduate. He also gave us a present; our day one patrolling assignments. I didn't get anything.

Packed by 2230. Ready to go. Turns out to be the only day since we've been here that we've eaten all three meals in the mess.

SLEEP: 152300—160430                    TOTAL: 5.5 Hours
                                        Missed Meals: none

## 16 JULY 1980 (Florida Phase: Day 44)

> **The execution of an enterprise is never equal to the conception of it in the confident mind of its promoter; for men are safe while they are forming plans but when the time of action comes, then they lose their presence of mind and fail.**
>
> Thucydides,
> THE PELOPONNESIAN WAR, c. 460 BC

Day 1 of our twelve-day patrol. After breakfast, we took a quick run over to the classroom for a final briefing that included a question and answer session. The temperature is still a scorcher at 100+ degrees. Because of this, our departure time through the friendly forward unit will not be until 1930. Excellent.

Our planning was conducted in an old hangar. The flies around here are eating us alive. I'm a team leader for today. Ate breakfast and lunch in garrison. There is really nothing for me to do but take it easy until we depart. Patrol is platoon size, approximately 40 to 45 Rangers.

The RIs conducted a shakedown prior to our departure. They went through everything—rucks and body—searching for pogie. Even the number of sticks of gum and lifesavers are regulated. Our RI only conducted a cursory check of our rucks. No body cavity searches— what a shame. Supposedly, anyone found with pogie will be tossed from the course or recycled back to Benning. That wasn't put to the test, though, for they found no pogie.

Departed the friendly forward unit. Conducted a stream crossing that was mid-thigh deep. We missed our assault time at the objective so our mission was fragged to a raid. The patrol leader really tied that one up.

Afterwards, as we moved from the objective area, we had to stop and ground our equipment because of an electrical storm. No rain, but it did provide us with an opportunity to grab a few (very few) winks.

SLEEP: none                        TOTAL: 0 Hours
                                          Missed Meals: D

## 17 JULY 1980 (Florida Phase: Day 45)

**Hesitation and half measures lose all in war.**

Napoleon,
MAXIMS OF WAR, 1831

Moved all night. Most everyone is already in a catatonic, drone state of mind. And to think that this is just the end of the first day. Ambushes all over. We had one by the trucks yesterday before we hit the objective rally point and two more tonight.

We could have had our own hasty ambush but our patrol leader missed the opportunity. The enemy patrol moved through our potential ambush site without a shot being fired. Upon reflection, our not initiating contact was probably the smartest move. In our condition, we probably would have had our butts whipped—even with surprise and superior numbers on our side.

Moved five clicks to our patrol base. Somehow these clicks seem longer than the mountain ones even though they are over level ground. Less energy left after the mountains to conduct the move, I suppose. Made the patrol base by 0600. Never would have made it in time cross-country. I carried the PRC77 on the road-march portion. Damn, did it ever cut into the ol' shoulders.

By 0800, our new RIs were on board. Stopped by the medic to have my fingers bandaged. They are still torn up pretty badly with all those rappelling blisters.

One good thing happened—our rucks were taken by truck to the objective. Of course, for every action there is an equal and opposite reaction. Today was no exception, for the patrol base was hit by a Special Forces unit. Continued to eat throughout their attack, though. Food is too precious at this stage to risk losing.

We moved out at 1100 on a long haul of seven clicks. Today was supposed to be an airmobile, but since no choppers are available, we will use the M1A1 multipurpose leather personnel carrier (LPC) boots.

While moving through a swampy area, one to two feet deep, we were joined by an unwelcome guest—a water moccasin. This three to four foot long reptile swam parallel to our track about ten feet away. It stayed with us for approximately five minutes. If it had moved on us, we'd have scattered like water bugs and sought the nearest tree to climb. Snakes ... they are everywhere. But they are probably as scared of us as we are of them.

It is definitely hot. The RIs made us sit in a stream while we conducted a patrol critique. Later, as we moved to another patrol base, we were ambushed twice along the way. Established our patrol base, planned, established our objective rally point, conducted a leader's recon, issued a frago, then conducted our assault.

SLEEP: 180200—180300                    TOTAL: 1 Hour
                                        Missed Meals: L D

## 18 JULY 1980 (Florida Phase: Day 46)

**Complaints have been brought to my attention that the infantry have got their feet wet. That is the fault of the weather. The march was made in the service of the most mighty monarch. Only women, dandies, and lazybones need good weather.**

> Field Marshal Prince Aleksandr V. Suvorov, 1799, to the commander of the Austrian allied force who complained of having to march in bad weather, quoted in Longworth, THE SCIENCE OF VICTORY, 1966

Conducted our critique immediately after the raid at 0001. Picked up our rucks and marched another three clicks to a patrol base. Ended up stopping half way and grounding our equipment during another electrical storm. Just like with the other storm, no rain. The storm was over before it started, but the RI let us sleep for about a hour.

Our movement tonight was pretty decent. Maybe there is a learning curve after all. Didn't feel quite as burnt out. Established our patrol base by 0530—in time for about forty minutes of sleep.

Ate breakfast as the RIs switched over at 0830. My index finger is definitely a nasty mess by now from my mountain phase rappelling blisters. We moved out early, around 0930, for two clicks to an aerial resupply drop zone. Ended up waiting there until 1330. Finally, they dropped our ammo and chow.

Avoided an ambush on our movement out of the area as we began a four-click journey. Walked through another stream, which makes absolutely no difference anymore. There is no way one can remain dry out here—between the rain, the heat, and the streams, which, I have no doubt, the RIs intentionally plan for us to cross on a daily basis. Ended up raining for about an hour. It's pretty neat watching the rain front advance through the trees towards you. I'm toting the M60 again, as usual.

During the early evening and night hours of our patrol, I hear the sound of C130s flying overhead and the cacophony of 105mm howitzers, 40mm Bofors, and miniguns firing—Specter Gunships. The RIs say they've been firing nearly every day for over a month. Part of an Iranian hostage rescue mission? At the moment, I just hope their target acquisition equipment is operating within specified parameters. I'd hate to see a wall of lead slicing through the air towards us one day. I have no desire to be on the receiving end of one of those flying arsenals. I'm terribly allergic to lead.

We arrived at the patrol base and shortly, thereafter, the objective rally point. We set up an ambush along a road by 2400. I was on the right support position with the M60. One of the Rangers in our support group got up and walked off in a daze. No one paid him much attention for we were all in our own fog. Then, another Ranger walked by. Thinking that we were moving out—did anyone question why we had yet to execute the ambush?—we rucked up and prepared to move. It was then that we noticed our sleepwalking Ranger's ruck was still on the ground with no body to go with it. Turned out he was roaming down the road along the assault line.

Moments later, it started to rain. Still milling about and realizing that we did not have a clue what we were doing, we elected to settle into our positions once again and pulled out our ponchos. Why we pulled them out, I do not know. We really don't care about being wet or filthy anymore. It's become such a natural state of affairs.

Our wayward, sleepwalking Ranger, whom we had tracked down and brought back into the fold earlier, was up and sleep walking for a second time tonight. We need to tie that poor boy down with a rope. It was funny as hell and served as a bit of comic relief. We are far past 'tracer burn-out' now. Fatigue has made us numb. To say we are catatonic would be stretching the truth somewhat. We are the living dead.

Everyone fell asleep on support or sat there in some mystical haze. Somehow, probably because of the noise of the vehicles, we awoke around 0300 just as enemy jeeps were moving in front of us. I had to take a few moments to clear the cobwebs and to figure out where my weapon was.

We initiated the ambush with "claymore" antipersonnel mines. I put 200 rounds on the objective with the M60. The weapon works well now after the helpful tips provided by one of the RIs to clean the gas piston.

Unfortunately, during the engagement, our support team was overrun by RI aggressors. We didn't have a clue as to what was going on as they ran by "blowing" us away. Where was security? The ambush was a bust. Having had our tails handed to us, we moved out for 1500 meters to establish a patrol base.

SLEEP: 190001—190300          TOTAL: 3 Hours

Missed Meals: L

## 19 JULY 1980 (Florida Phase: Day 47)

> **Those who do not know the conditions of mountains and forests, hazardous defiles, marshes and swamps, cannot conduct the march of an army. Those who do not use local guides are unable to obtain the advantages of the ground.**
>
> Sun Tzu,
> THE ART OF WAR, c. 500 BC

The day started out well but from there, we progressively began to lose ground. We left the patrol base at 0930. As soon as we left, it began to pour and thunder. Ominous. We went to a RB15 site and grounded our gear there until the lightning cleared the area.

We launched our boats for a fifteen-click ride down the river. Certainly better than humping that distance. The camp commander was with our boat. Upon hitting our landing site, we moved through an ankle high, mucky portion of swamp for 700 meters—great workout for the legs—to an objective rally point site on an island. Large clumps of grass all about.

From the objective rally point, we moved into an assault line to attack a building. It was not my idea of a quiet movement, breaking through the jungle growth every step of the way. We must have sounded like a heard of elephants.

At 2000, we assaulted the objective. The M60 jammed for its gunner so I took it over. We've become very intimate friends, that M60 "pig" and I. Pulled a "John Wayne" with over 200 rounds. Definitely Hollywood ... standing up, belts of ammo draped all over me like Frito Bandito for which I'd already been dropped for pushups before… firing with one hand while I fed rounds into the weapon with the other. For those who do not think so, there are some lighter moments in the course. What a hot dog!

After a critique on the objective, we moved off into the swamp at 2200. Little did we realize the terror that would soon engulf us. With the double canopy above us in addition to the overcast conditions, it was as dark as it has ever been.

When entering a swamp, one is supposed to maintain a straight azimuth through it. Did we do that? Of course not. At the rear of the Ranger file, I looked ahead and saw the cat eyes veer off at a right angle. This would prompt the RI to let out with a severe tongue lashing of the patrol leader for, of course, if we were lost in the swamp so was the RI. Was this the self-preservation function kicking in? These tongue lashings made no difference for the patrol leader and compass man ended up taking us all over hell's half acre, anyway. We were still marching past midnight, staggering over tree stumps and through wait-a-minute-vines. We were calf deep in muck but, unbeknownst to us, the best was yet to come.

SLEEP: none                                                     TOTAL: 0 Hours
                                                                                Missed Meals: L D

## 20 JULY 1980 (Florida Phase: Day 48)

**We will either find a way or make one.**

Hannibal

What pure hell! If there's any consolation, it's the fact that in the future, should anyone tell me to go to hell, I can now say in all honesty, "I've been there!"

Four hours into this quagmire, we struck pay dirt with a real swamp, Florida style. At first, we had the muck. Then we had ankle deep water. Progressively, as we continued to drive on, the water's depth increased until it was above our waists. What a trip. Rangers were crashing and burning everywhere as we staggered over and through underwater stumps, vines, roots, and quicksand.

Around 0230, we had to stop for a one-rope bridge crossing of a large creek in the middle of the swamp! All of our class' patrols hit the crossing site at the same time. Our patrol pulled guard as another patrol erected the bridge, which meant some other poor souls would have to strip down to the buff and swim to the far side to anchor the bridge or to provide security.

Rather than sit in the water, I did a quick 360 degree sweep of the area with my red-lensed flashlight, located a tree stump sticking out of the water, and perched in it like a bird just as the rain began again. Now, I'm ready to quit. The only problem is I still have to walk out of this damn place. Ahhh ... All of a sudden, I heard all of these plop, plops. Taking the red lens off my flashlight and shielding its beam, I looked about me and was amazed to find nothing but heads awash, floating above the water! The rest of the squad had gone into a rucksack flop and were dead asleep, with only their heads above the water. Yes, sir. Where there is a will, there is a way.

Well ... to make a long story short, we all fell asleep. The next thing I recall was hearing a voice, off in the distance, screaming for the lost squad in third platoon. That was us, of course. It was an RI at the crossing site. Everyone else had crossed except for us, and now they were trying to track us down. Somehow, we got everyone awake, located all of the equipment and weapons that had fallen underwater, and moved to the bridge—all without a clue as to what we were doing.

Once on the other side of the river, it only got worse. As we continued to move, the water continued to increase in depth until it was up to our necks. For those with a little less height, forget it. They were already underwater. The muck underneath was grabbing at our calves while the water above it was doing its best to enter our stomachs and lungs. Those who were 'rock squaders'—as in non-swimming personnel—had to be looked after and were marked with extra cat-eyes on their PCs. Most of them were placed forward in the formation and were required to have little lanterns attached to their web gear—to aid underwater searches?

The Ranger in front of me was in a significant hurt. He could not swim and he was short. I spent many a moment with the M60 wrapped around my neck and one hand on a Cyprus tree root as I reached under the water with the other to pull him back to the surface and throw him forward in the direction of another tree. 'Walking' in the rut created by the 120+ Rangers who had tread before us, those of us at the rear of the movement had to resort to the 'bob and travel' mode of self propulsion. This technique required us to duck under the water and push off in a forward direction of movement. I almost cried, but it was too funny. Now THIS is Ranger School!

Finally, at 0600, we hauled our waterlogged, nasty carcasses out of the swamp—eight hours after entering it. One moment we were walking under water, the next we were scrambling up an eight-foot embankment onto terra firma. The rain had let up a bit during the last hours of our movement but picked up in intensity as we exited.

We moved another two clicks by road to our patrol base. This is definitely the definition of misery.

Our new RIs appear to be excellent. It continues to rain, alternating between heavy and moderate. Over a third of the company is on sick call for immersion foot or immersion hand. It's been raining on us for two straight days now. Everyone is a mess. During the course of checking on my squad, one of the RIs ordered me on sick call. My hands are a disaster. My rappelling blisters have all broken, leaving the raw meat below exposed. Combine that with the die from my black leather outer shell gloves that I wear during movements and the 42 hours or so of being soaked ... well you get the picture. They are downright disgusting. As to when I last slept ... I believe it was two and a half days ago if my notes are correct. Oh, yes. We're having some fun now.

The Field Marshall, however, was having an even better time of it...with immersion testicles. Holding his "jewels" in one hand and his rifle in the other, he tried in vain to stop the chaffing as he crossed the swamp. And I thought I had it bad with my hands?

Finally, a miracle. The exercise was called; too many Rangers on sick call. At 1300, our Ranger class was trucked back to Auxiliary Field 6. We cleaned up, received medical attention, and ate. Many of us were placed on rest tonight by the medics. Unfortunately, I was not one of them.

While at the aid station, our greatest entertainment proved to be seeing who could pull the largest single piece of dead skin off the bottom of his feet. We also found it to be a neat phenomenon to stick needles into our feet and not be able to feel anything. Masochistic and abnormal, huh?

The RIs are rather disturbed with our class. They are not very pleased by the fact we returned to garrison. Hopefully, they will realize that we were not consulted about the decision to come in. That decision was made echelons above us.

By 1930, we were on the road again as we were trucked out to our demarcation point. I was point man. Our feet are wet, again, as we started off with a creek crossing. Actually, we crossed two of them in short order. We moved three clicks to the objective rally point. Our mission was to conduct an ambush but our start was not very auspicious for we immediately lost two of our patrol members who had fallen asleep. We ended up wasting an hour and a half tracking them down, expending what seemed to be a few tons of artillery simulators and star clusters in an attempt to wake them up or illuminate their bodies.

We gave up on the ambush and moved to a patrol base by road. Everyone was falling asleep. The RIs took no pity and failed everyone who was in the chain-of-command. The RIs stated in no uncertain terms that this was the worst patrol they'd ever seen. While they probably say that to everyone at this stage, this time they just might be right. It was not a very pretty sight.

SLEEP: none                                          TOTAL: 0 Hours
                                                     Missed Meals: L D

## 21 JULY 1980 (Florida Phase: Day 49)

**Understand that the foundation of an army is the belly. It is necessary to procure nourishment for the soldier wherever you assemble him and wherever you wish to conduct him. This is the primary duty of a general.**

Frederick the Great,
INSTRUCTIONS TO HIS GENERALS, 1747

Still thinking about last night on point. I ran, face first, into more damn spiders! Their webs are almost as tough as rope. It also turned out that a night vision device was lost last night. The Ranger who lost it and the student chain-of-command had to go out and look for it. Fortunately for him, and us, they found it.

Today is survival training day. We had the morning off which provided us an opportunity to lounge about with our boots off—and pretty much everything else, also. The morning started off nicely, weather-wise, then changed to rain off and on. Mac and I tried to sleep under a poncho but we did not have much success.

Finally, at 1200, we began classes on traps and the killing of chickens, rabbits, and snakes. The RIs also did an excellent skit about Ranger hallucinations that involved a "Coca-Cola" tree. As time goes on in the course, one has a tendency to start seeing things, especially food. The RIs skit was about a Ranger student who "saw" a Coke machine while on patrol. The real kicker was when the "student" reached behind the tree and pulled out an ice-cold can of Coke, popped the tab, and guzzled it before our haggard eyes. Oh the pain! Most of us would have considered selling our souls for just one swig of that sweet nectar.

By 1600, our squad was given two live chickens, two live rabbits, seven fish (floaters—as in dead), and an assortment of vegetables, apples, tea, and rice. We didn't have the heart to kill the rabbits so we let them go. They were pretty scrawny, anyway. I ended up killing one of the chickens. I stroked its neck for a while to calm it down—supposedly the meat is tougher if the adrenaline is pumping—and then popped its head off in one smooth motion. Painless or so it seems, never having experienced it myself. I now know what they mean by the adage, "running around like a chicken with its head cut-off," for it took over a minute for the body to finally stop moving. I must admit it was a very strange feeling placing my hand into the warm body cavity of something that, only moments before, had been alive. It's enough to make one pause and consider the meaning of death and mortality.

Anyway, the meal was good, or maybe it was just our hunger. Whatever, it proved to be an easy day and an easy night.

SLEEP: 212130—220500          TOTAL: 7.5 Hours
                              Missed Meals: B L

## 22 JULY 1980 (Florida Phase: Day 50)

> Probably one of the greatest assets a commander can have is the ability to radiate confidence in the plan and operations even (perhaps especially) when inwardly he is not too sure about the outcome.
> Field Marshal Viscount Montgomery of Alamein,
> THE MEMOIRS OF
> FIELD MARSHAL MONTGOMERY

Ugh. Feel rotten. Too much sleep and (or) food from yesterday. Hungry as hell now, though; starving actually. The ole rennin and pepsin stomach acids are putting in overtime. We moved out and set up a patrol base.

Our new RIs came on board. No chain-of-command spot yet. This is really beginning to grate on my nerves. Many others have already had their second shot at getting a Go. I have yet to have my first. What gives? I want that one to Tab out. I'm in a real crabby mood, snapping at everyone. By the time I get my opportunity, everyone will have attained tracer burnout. Great. Talk about being caught between a rock and a hard place.

Ate some crackers, a vanilla fudge bar, and am writing this to get by. My mind's on food, big time now. The weather stinks but nothing new there. It's been raining on and off all morning. We're drenched. In other words, situation normal. My Ranger Buddy is the patrol leader. That should mean kick back time for me.

We departed the patrol base at 1700 and moved five clicks to an objective rally point. At 2130, my Ranger Buddy is relieved as patrol leader and yours truly is now it. This whole mission has been trouble from the start. We're lost. Everyone the RI asked, to include the previous PL and APL, did not know where they were. Only by accident do I know. Out of sheer boredom and dreaded anticipation, I happened to trace our movement on my map.

Our mission was to attack a bridge by 2400. The problem was we still had another click and a half to go and we had less than two and a half hours to do it in. In that, extensions are a luxury not granted and I had to make up for lost time. I had no choice but to break every tactical rule to accomplish the mission. I issued a quick frago, took the point, and told the RI to follow me because nothing was going to be done by the book on this movement. Ignoring noise discipline and establishing flank security on the move as we crossed danger areas without stopping, we quickly moved to establish an objective rally point by force.

Arriving at the objective rally point at 2345 and having no time to conduct a leader's recon, I quickly moved (ran) the patrol down a trail towards the objective. It's amazing the energy one finds when he feels the world slipping out of his hands. We turned a corner of the trail and laid eyes on the objective with one minute to spare. I placed a security element back along the trail we just came down and another up the road leading to the objective bridge.

At 2400, the support team opened up. Minutes later, as our assault was overrunning the bridge, an RI convoy consisting of a 5-ton cargo truck and two jeeps, all with mounted M60's, came down the road with weapons firing and ran into one of our two security teams.

While this firefight was going on up the road, we were on the bridge that was stacked with cases of C-rats. When some Rangers asked what we should do since there had been no mention in our Operations Order of food, I thought it was quite obvious what we should do; take the damn food! One never passes up an opportunity to eat. When in doubt, take. Turned out to be exactly enough for two C-rats per man.

I later found out that the Field Marshall's patrol had an identical mission…but rather than grab the C-rats…they left them behind…given that they had not been part of the OPORD. Later, in their ORP, there was a near mutiny when the RI told them they'd have to go without eating because they had not secured and brought them back with them. Realizing that such a stand was not the smartest with a group of 40+ starving Ranger students looking on, the RI relented and allowed them to return to the OBJ to pick them up.

As for our motley crew, with C-rats in hand, we began to move back down the trail we had traveled from our objective rally point. The tactic was unsound but we had no choice. Unfortunately, the movement was right into a near ambush that the RIs had set up right next to one of my security teams. Turned out the RIs had browbeat the security team firing up their vehicles into telling where our objective rally point was. Then the RIs moved dismounted through the woods and set up this nice reception as my other security team slept. Nice touch.

Well … when faced with a near ambush, what does one do? You attack it directly, of course, which we proceeded to do. The only problem was that there was a large quantity of old concertina and barbed wire between us and the ambush that proved to be just a tad bit difficult to see at 0030 in the morning. I ended up with a number of bodies twitching and entangled in the wire as the 'lead' and 'artillery' rained all about us.

My fun meter was now pegged. Actually, it was wrapped around the post. Yelling at the RI that I had enough of this bullshit, I told him that I was calling an admin halt to this fiasco—a pretty ballsy move, if I do say so myself. Besides, my first fire team had engaged and killed these same RIs earlier. For all intents and purposes, they were dead to me. With the RIs still firing us up, I gathered up the patrol, placed them on the trail, and began to move towards the objective rally point once again.

About 200 meters later, the RIs opened up with another ambush, but I refused to play that game. We just kept shuffling along as the RIs attempted to engage us. Finally, at the objective rally point, we distributed the C-rats, disseminated information, and prepared for our movement to a patrol base.

Prior to departing on a leader's recon of the patrol base, I left specific orders with my assistant patrol leader as to what I wanted accomplished prior to my return. Problem was, my assistant patrol leader was a recycle. We think we are beat after this training? What do you think someone feels like after they've been through the same phase twice? I just wish I had thought of that prior to my departure from the objective rally point.

Moving out with the recon element, we moved approximately two clicks with me as point and compass man. I wasn't taking any chances. If I were to fail, it was to be because of my ineptitude, not someone else's. After establishing the patrol base, I stopped by the Ranger located at the 6 o'clock position and warned him to remain awake for I would need him to guide me in when I returned with the remainder of the patrol. "No problem" was his response. Ha! If I had only thought about it. He was a recycle, too, a 2LT. Stay awake? Not on your life—or my Tab for that matter.

Returning on my own, I linked back up with the main body. Of course, my APL did everything ass backwards of what I had directed. Getting it all squared away cost another ten to fifteen minutes.

We hit the woods with me as pace and compass man, again. Two clicks later, I was where I believed the patrol base to be, but no Rangers. Great. There I was standing in the middle of the woods, apparently lost with 30+ Rangers while my other 12 Rangers were out there somewhere. Moments later, when I'd just about lost all hope, a message was passed up the Ranger file to me that there was a body lying on the ground next our file. Turns out that I had walked right by my 6 o'clock "No problem" Ranger and I was now standing in the center of the patrol base.

Frustration, anger, and lack of sleep took over at this point as I pictured the Coveted Black and Gold slipping out of my grasp and flying off into the star-lit sky. I barely recall moving back to where the body was lying on the ground and drop kicking him as I let loose with a boot to the ribs. At the last possible moment, I held back on the force of the kick—a trace of discipline or sanity? But it still proved to be a good shot, for it lifted him off the ground and sent him rolling and screaming. I grabbed him by the collar, lifted him off the ground, and slammed him up against a tree as I proceeded to slap him a number of times while cursing his ancestors—so much for noise discipline.

Finally, after a few moments, I was able to gather some self-control. As he lay crumpled on the ground—fortunately for him and for me, he had no serious or permanent injuries, I turned and faced the rest of the patrol who were just standing there with stunned looks on their faces. In the distance, I could hear the NCO RI laughing.

I proceeded to threaten everyone with the same treatment if they did not listen up and begin following orders. Not exactly the best way to make friends and influence people—it seems as though that lesson learned about peers and tact had not taken completely.

One last confrontation had me nose to chest—for this Ranger was about six inches taller than I and outweighed me by about 25 pounds— with another who, after some stiff finger jabs to the chest from me, decided that semi-crazed, non-Tabbed-out Rangers were somewhat unstable and not worth the risk of confronting.

Eventually, things did settle down as everyone hit the ground and began to power down. Unfortunately, all was not over yet for the RIs called in a B-52 "strike" in the vicinity that required us to dig foxholes.

Prior to the patrol critique, the Ranger Camp XO, a Vietnam vet captain who was serving as one of the RIs, sat me down to evaluate my performance—or lack, thereof. When asked by him as to what I thought of the evening's adventures, I responded by saying that this patrol was the worst one I'd been on to date—to include Les', which is saying a hell of a lot. Much to my surprise, he said that while some of my techniques were indeed a bit unorthodox or primitive, the patrol was successful despite one of my fellow Rangers breaking light discipline a few hours earlier by starting a fire to heat his meal—of all the things to nearly fail me. But, then again, I can't say that I strictly adhered to the standards of noise discipline, either. Bottom line: Lock was a Go at this station. Yes ... Tabbed out!

The patrol critique, itself, proved to be rather entertaining also. It was a classic "Me vs. The World" confrontation. I sat on one side, the rest of the patrol on the other, while the RIs refereed in the middle. When we got to the patrol base activities, the large Ranger whom I had stood toe to toe with earlier stood up and rather emphatically stated that I had no right to do what I did. I came back with the insightful response that he was lucky I hadn't kicked his ass. Ah, Lock, you ol' silver tongue devil; such witty repartee.

Somehow, the RIs smoothed it all over and the group consensus was not to tar and feather me and ride me out of the swamp on a log.

SLEEP: none                                      TOTAL: 0 Hours
                                                             Missed Meals: L D

## 23 JULY 1980 (Florida Phase: Day 51)

**Nothing undermines morale more decisively than hunger; quickest of all is the effect of any digestive upset. That was strikingly demonstrated in the late summer of 1918, when the morale slump of the German troops became most marked at a moment when stomach disorders, due to bad food, were rife among them. The old saying that 'an army**

marches on its stomach' has a wider and deeper application than has yet been given to it. An army fights on its
stomach, and falls if its stomach is upset.

> Captain Sir Basil Liddell Hart,
> THOUGHTS ON WAR, 1944

It rained all morning, again. At first, early in the course, it felt quite uncomfortable to be wet and dirty. But, as the days progress and the normal state of affairs was to be wet, filthy, and miserable, it feels abnormal to be dry or clean.

We planned all morning at the patrol base and moved out at 1300 for the pickup zone. Airmobile, yeah. Finally, choppers. They arrived at 1500 to take us on a quick flight of 25 clicks.

Rumor had it that the pilots really take pity on Ranger students—could be because the pilots from Fort Rucker are students themselves—and dole out pogie. The rumor turned out to be fact. Riding by myself on the starboard side, I was handed a huge bag of chocolate chip cookies and fruit. Seems to be a traditional thing. The RIs appear to overlook the food—for the most part—as long as none of it gets off the aircraft with you. The only exception appeared to be if they were on the bird with you. The rumor through our student grape-vine was that the Rangers in aircraft with RIs on board had no pogie. Now, there's a tough break.

It doesn't take long to travel 25 clicks at 100+ mph, therefore, you inhale the food as best you can. Twelve cookies and two huge, juicy, red apples later, we hit the landing zone. Not bad. The worst part, though, was that the route took us over Eglin Air Force Base. Cars, houses, buildings, people—civilization. A world truly did still exist outside of our own. It was akin to viewing paradise.

We set down at the landing zone, quickly off loaded, and established a security perimeter until the choppers took off. With each beat of their retreating blades, a wave of depression rose until it crashed over us with the disappearance of the last audible decibel. For a few moments, we just stood around staring at each other, really wondering if it had all been real.

Even with all the Rangers standing about, it was the loneliest of feelings. But, there was a mission to accomplish and the objective rally point was only 1500 meters away.

Our leader's recon was compromised and the objective rally point was attacked by trackers. Despite all of this, we moved to the assault line at 1900, overran the objective, moved out of the area, then stopped and conducted a critique.

New mission: conduct an ambush in the vicinity of a dam site. The location was only one click away. The ambush was initiated at 2300. It was a good ambush. All of the M60s even fired. Ah, music to our ears.

Moved 3K to our patrol base. What a haul. Everyone is burnt out. Humping the PRC77 for most of the way certainly did not help my cause, and of course, there was the usual swamp and creek requirement to meet—waist deep and cold. We finally made it to the patrol base at 0400. Unfortunately, with priorities and stand-to, there was no sleep.

Food is now an obsession. Especially strawberry shortcakes. I never would have believed this before but I can literally taste it when I fantasize about one—which is quite often. I wonder if I'm putting on any weight?

SLEEP: none                                    TOTAL: 0 Hours
                                               Missed Meals: L D

## 24 JULY 1980 (Florida Phase: Day 52)

**It is right to be very concerned about the wounded. If we neglect them, we will find the rest of the troops will deliberately not fight well, and our remissness will cause us to lose some who could have been saved.**

> The Emperor Maurice,
> THE STRATEGIKON, c. AD 600

Graduation is only one week away. Unfortunately, that is not much of a motivator at the moment, for I feel like shit today. Burn out city. I almost turned into a drone last night. Ate breakfast this morning though there is no difference between breakfast, lunch, and dinner meals other than the time they are consumed. I always feel better afterwards. I wonder when we'll start hallucinating about the 'Coke' trees?

Our new RIs were early today, arriving at 0700. Fifteen minutes later we were moving out. I've joined back up with my good buddy, again, the M60. We moved 3K to an objective rally point to conduct a partisan link-up. While the patrol leader was gone to affect the link-up, an RI brought in artillery on us and created wounded in the process. We had to abandon the objective rally point, carrying and providing 'medical' assistance to our wounded on the move. Finally, we were able to move back to the objective rally point.

When the patrol leader returned, we moved out through another swamp and creek—though these were not so bad—to another patrol base about 1K away, arriving around 1300. Turns out the link-up was a failure. The partisan woman spoke only in Spanish. None of the Rangers could translate. Consequently, she drove off, laughing, not having passed any information. Nice touch. The score was RIs: 1, Ranger students: 0.

Later, I found out that Les had a similar experience as patrol leader. Fortunately for him, he was able to access the far reaches of his memory core and dredge up some classroom Spanish. Unfortunately, he never was very fluent in the language. The partisan's opening remark was "It looks like rain today" to which Les responded "Does your mother like to dance?" Obviously, his translation left a little to be desired. I think it's what could be termed a lack of communication.

We moved out from the patrol base at 1900 with me as compass/point man. The objective rally point was 2K away. It was a good time. We were ambushed on the trail and the whole patrol fell apart. We were blown away. I was killed while crossing a road and ended up having my body carried for a distance. Rangers don't leave their own. Why didn't they kill someone a little lighter? The ambush cost us an hour.

We finally made it to the objective rally point but we were a bit late. The leader's recon was supposed to be finished by 2100. We never got to it until 2230.

We were to return to our billets for a quick break after the patrol.

Link-up with the friendly forward unit was supposed to be at 2330. We didn't make it until 2400. It feels great to see civilization, even if it is a military installation.

Conducted our critique until 0100. Showered, ate a box lunch. Excellent for once. Or is it simply because we'll eat anything now? Hit the rack. Ah. How do you spell relief? S-L-E-E-P.

SLEEP: 250230—050630                    TOTAL: 4 Hours
                                                    Missed Meals: L

## 25 JULY 1980 (Florida Phase: Day 53)

**Remember, gentlemen, an order that can be misunderstood will be misunderstood.**
Field Marshal Helmuth Graf von Moltke
(1800-1891)

Up at 0630, breakfast at 0700. Hot A's. Somewhat of a rushed morning. The camp commander talked to us, saying that the company was hurting. To date, there were only 60 Goes. Not even 50 percent of the class.

Well, it's off to the jungle again. We linked up with our RIs to initiate plans for our new mission. The RIs will not let us use the hangar to plan. Ended up walking a ways to establish a patrol base for planning purposes. This provided me an opportunity to go on sick call to have my feet looked at. They were still hurting from immersion foot and the beating they took in the mountains.

It also gave me an opportunity to pick up my clothes from the laundry room. Turns out some kind soul had dried them for me. To whomever, thanks. I had been forced to leave them in the washer when we departed. I went up into the billets, repacked my ruck, and headed back to the patrol base ready to go.

At the patrol base, the airborne personnel were going through prejump in preparation for an airborne operation at 2030. We legs just laid around for the rest of day taking it easy. There are definitely some advantages to being a dirty, nasty leg.

We moved to the drop zone (DZ) at 1900 to wait for the airborne insertion of the airborne Rangers. While lying in wait, I examined some huge grasshoppers that were out and about. Chocolate covered, anyone? They're high in protein.

At 2030, two C130's appeared overhead and spewed forth their cargo. Must admit it was an impressive sight. Once everyone assembled, we moved off to an objective rally point five clicks away. There was a full moon and visibility was great. Unfortunately, the patrol leader's plan was not as clear as the visibility that evening. When he emplaced the support group for supporting fires on the objective, he told them to prep the target with fires at 0045 but left them with no means to communicate. He then returned to the objective rally point to gather the assault force. Then Murph showed up. The support team opened fire while we were still in the patrol base. We ended up running 150 meters to the objective, through our support team's fire. What a mess.

After overrunning the objective, we pulled back. At this point, I took one of the M60s for the 2.5K movement. There was the potential for a one-rope bridge crossing, but the RIs took pity on us—and by extension themselves—by showing us where we could cross without a rope. The river was only waist deep but it was nasty. We finally hit the patrol base around 0300.

We are the walking dead, now. The chain-of-command is fighting for their lives because they are all down either without a Go or less than 50 percent overall. Unfortunately, they came into the patrol base with Goes and ended up with No Goes because everyone self-destructed once we settled into the patrol base: Rangers falling asleep, priorities not being accomplished. As a class, we will undoubtedly have an extremely low passing rate.

SLEEP: none                                    TOTAL: 0 Hours
                                               Missed Meals: L D

## 26 JULY 1980 (Florida Phase: Day 54)

**The sword is the soul of the warrior. If any forget or lose it, he will not be excused.**

Tokugawa Ieyasu (1543-1616), quoted in Sadler
THE MAKER OF MODERN JAPAN

Only one more day to go after today. The last night out. The new RIs joined us at 0800. We picked up and moved at 0820 to a new patrol base 3K away. I am currently a team leader. The weather is very radical. One moment sunshine, the next a downpour. I cannot remember the last time I was dry.

My team went to set up a listening post (LP). Rain again. Since we were on 50 percent security, I thought it would be safe to sleep as long as two others remained awake. Wrong assumption. What is it they say about the word "assume"? It makes an ASS out of U and ME? It sure does. Within minutes, we were all fast asleep. One of the team members even fell asleep while heating up his food. Incredible. Everyone wonders why I don't sleep on the perimeter? This is why. You cannot trust anyone to stay awake—everyone achieved tracer burnout long ago. I've had enough major minus spots to keep me borderline. I cannot afford any more.

Well, as is par for the course, an RI caught us asleep, took one of our weapons, and shot us all dead. He made the patrol leader carry us back to the patrol base where a burial ceremony, complete with eulogy, was conducted. Six foot deep graves were dug and we were lowered, or should I say, tossed in. The RI even had them throw some dirt in on top of us. Damn, was I ever fit to be tied. It was humiliating to have to lie there. I think I drew blood on my lip having to bite it so hard to keep my mouth shut. (Note: While preparing this book for publication, another very successful author who was also a Ranger School graduate mentioned to me that he had an opportunity to observe a 'burial' scene similar to the one I described. He had written about the experience and had forwarded me a copy. I was struck by our differences in perspective. While he had reflected as a student on the consequences of poor leaders—as in 'burying' one's mistakes, I had fumed on the consequences and humiliation suffered as a result of sleeping classmates. I must admit upon reflection that I preferred his perspective over mine.)

With the 'services' completed, we extracted ourselves from our graves and moved out at 1700 to our objective rally point 3K away. We arrived around 1900, at which time we were hit by aggressors. Our raid on a road network at 2100 went pretty well.

After the raid, we moved 4K to another patrol base. Arriving at 2400, we had to dig chest high, two-man fighting positions. The ground was mostly sand and there were old, filled-in foxholes in the area which we quite obviously took advantage of. To keep us entertained, the rain continued to come and go rather routinely.

Turns out that a Ranger lost an M60. He couldn't even recall if he had brought it into the patrol base with him. After a fruitless thirty-minute search of the immediate area, the RI let out with some curses and launched a kick at a pile of sand next to the Ranger's foxhole. Moments later, we picked the injured RI up off the ground. Lo and behold, he had found the M60. It was buried under the pile of sand! Amazing. How did he know it was there?

Around 0300, the aggressors hit. They opened up with M60s and artillery. Our contingency plan was to move out of the perimeter and through a swamp for 1K to a rally point. Unfortunately, there was one thing about the plan that I did not like—I was the point/compass man.

We broke from the perimeter in a mad rush with me leading and the aggressors in hot pursuit. Once again, leading with my face, I broke trail for the patrol. Staggering over, through, and around trees and bushes, I fought nature's elements with the greatest challenge coming from those damn jungle spiders.

With no time to reach forward and tear down a spider web, I had to go through many of them face first. It is amazing how tough they are to break through. I'd hit it at a pretty good speed, get held up by it, and usually have to spin and drive myself backwards through it. Then, stumbling about the place, I'd have to get my bearings, pick up the pace, try to rip the web off my face and patrol cap, and fight off the spider that I had taken by surprise as I assaulted its home. Those damn things seemed to be nearly as large as my hand and came in a multitude of radiant colors. The end result would usually be a screaming and cussing Ranger bouncing off trees and brush while engaging in mortal hand to face combat with a killer spider. It must have looked hilarious.

Finally, at 0400 and with my upper body literally covered in white from the spider webs, we arrived at our new patrol base.

SLEEP: 270200—270300          TOTAL: 1 Hour
                                          Missed Meals: L D

## 27 JULY 1980 (Florida Phase: Day 55)

**Nothing will throw an infantry attack off stride as quickly as to promise it support which is not precisely delivered both in time and volume.**

                Brigadier General S.L.A. Marshall,
                    MEN AGAINST FIRE

THIS IS IT! The final day of the patrol. I'm in great spirits (obviously) even though I'm wet and covered with spider cobwebs from our odyssey through the swamp. The RIs are coming down hard on the grading; certainly harder than they did for the first six days. They are giving out mostly No Goes now, which, for the most part, are earned. There is no doubt that the class' pass record will be pretty abysmal.

We ended up doing a lot of walking today. We started out at 0930 with a movement through a swamp to an objective rally point at the beach. The East Bay Swamp. Ugh. What a bear. Even movements during the day through swamps are miserable. Toted the M60 all day. The swamp water still smells like a urinal and the wait-a-minute vines are all over. The only good thing about the swamp was that it only ran from ankle to thigh depth and the water was cold for a hot day. Ended up sinking six to twelve inches with each step.

Our objective, a bridge, was 2K from the objective rally point and the assault fell apart. The enemy lit us up as did our own support element that killed about half of our assaulting force. Additionally, the

RIs took care of the support element with a grenade—probably because we were all herded together like sheep. Dead again.

From the objective, we moved to a bridging site. During the movement, we were blown away in a third platoon ambush on a road. While we were being slaughtered by friendlies, a third patrol was putting up a one-rope bridge. By the time we arrived at the crossing site, the bridge was completed which allowed us to cross quickly. The water was exceptionally deep with a swamp on both sides that was thigh deep. Those needing water would leave their canteen caps off and refill them as we crossed the stream.

We continued south on our movement through the swamp. No matter what, there always seems to be more swamp. Ended up moving for about 1K through it. For some reason, it always seems to be so much more.

We exited the swamp at a clearing just in time to hit another. This one was a bit different, though, for it was only a few feet deep for 200 meters and consisted of a grove of trees. The water was hot, having been warmed by the sun. Most of the movement was fun, for the chain of command ignored most of the danger areas we encountered. Should be No Go city, again.

We finally broke out into a clearing and established an objective rally point at 1500. We were only 700 meters from the beach—civilization and the end of this nightmare.

At 1900, weather change number 19 for today occurred. Another cloudburst. Nice and cold; miserable. We moved out at 1930 to the beach, crossing a highway as we approached. The off and on rain canceled our RB15 amphibious assault on the Gulf of Mexico island of Santa Rosa. The winds and surf were too high.

The patrol leader still needed a grade so an ambush was planned for 2200. We moved to the objective site, set up the ambush, and executed the mission.

After the mission, the RIs said we had to move through a swamp to another patrol base over 5K away. Truth or fiction? "Is it live or is it Memorex?" Moments later, cargo trucks showed up. We loaded up and headed back to garrison.

Upon arrival at Auxiliary Field 6, we dropped off our extra ammo and pyrotechnics at the hanger. Then we were searched, "No brass, no ammo," or something to that effect. The platoon critique was a blood bath. To say that our actions apparently left a little to be desired was an understatement.

Mac was a No Go. Hard to believe. Definitely feel badly for him— especially with no chance to recycle. USMA will not allow that. Not enough time to recover afterwards. Turns out two of Mac's three patrol failures were because of the inactions or incompetence of others. On one patrol, a POW team consisting of two cadets and a 2LT, fell asleep and let a partisan walk in and out of a trap. On the other patrol, a 2LT fell asleep while carrying an M60 with its selector switch off safe and let loose with a burst of noise and flame. Definitely a light and noise infraction, but one that is tough to defend against.

The bottom line is you do as much as YOU personally can do to accomplish and guarantee the success of the mission for, if you do not, someone else's oversight or incompetence stands a good chance of tubing your patrol.

As events would later have it, Johnny Mac would once again get his chance after graduation from USMA. Newly married and newly commissioned, he had to undertake the entire course again. His second time around proved to be the "charm" for he not only earned the Tab, he was also his class' Honor Graduate. Hoo Ahh.

SLEEP: 280200—280500         TOTAL: 2.5 Hours
(minus 1/2 hour guard)         Missed Meals: none

*****

## IT'S ALL OVER NOW!

*****

## 28 JULY 1980 (Florida Phase: Day 56)

> There is no quicker way to lose a battle than to lose it on the
> road for lack of adequate hardening of the troops. Such a
> condition cannot be redeemed by the resolve of a commander
> who insists on driving troops an extra mile beyond their gen-
> eral level of endurance. Extremes of this sort make men re-
> bellious and hateful of command, and thus strike at tactical
> efficiency from two directions at once. For when men resent
> a commander, they will not fight as willingly for him, and
> when their bodies are spent, their nerves are gone. In this
> state, the soldier's every act is mechanical. He is reduced to
> that automatism of mind which destroys his physical response.
> His courage is killed. His intellect falls asleep.
>
> Brigadier General S.L.A. Marshall,
> MEN AGAINST FIRE, 1947

Nothing much today. After breakfast we did Peer Reports, Florida critiques, and supply turn-in. Weighed in at 15 pounds under weight. That means I lost 17 pounds in the jungle phase. Some lost up to 40 to 45 pounds. As usual, it rained heavily for awhile this morning.

After lunch, if you can believe this, we had a PT Test. Unreal. The RIs did not mention this until after we ate so most of us were bloated. We did pushups, sit-ups, and a two-mile run on a steaming, hot, blacktop paved road. What a joke; we can barely move, much less run. Supposedly the Army is establishing the standards for a new Army Physical Fitness Test (APFT) and they are using burned out Rangers to determine the minimum standard. Well, minimum is what they got.

At 1600, we had our Super Supper. Afterwards, we had PX and phone privileges. Later, we all hung out in the Gator Lounge NCO Club. Tired as hell. Can barely keep my eyes open. I finished packing and then drifted off to sleep.

SLEEP: 282200—290001                    TOTAL: 2 Hours

                                         Missed Meals: none

## 29 JULY 1980 (Florida Phase: Day 57)

**Murphy's Law: anything that can go wrong, will go wrong.
Corollary to Murphy's Law: Murphy was an optimist.**

Up at midnight. Feel and look like hell. We finished packing and cleaning the billets by 0200. Afterwards, we waited for the buses to return us to Benning. The only problem was there were no buses. Turns out they were canceled by someone at Benning who thought we wouldn't be back until tomorrow. Obviously, the individual never heard of something called a phone or training schedule? We waited on the concrete, in the hot sun until 1300. So much for our 12-hour break.

We finally arrived at Benning around 1800. As a consolation for our missed break, we were given PX and phone privileges. We spent all night cleaning equipment and prepping it for turn-in.

This is now my second day of intense stomach disorder. The damn thing feels overextended. I can't believe it; after all of this, my stomach has finally let me down.

SLEEP: 300100—300400 TOTAL: 3 Hour
Missed Meals: none

# FLORIDA PHASE

*Eglin Air Force Base, Auxiliary Field 6...the Florida Ranger Camp. Relatively comfortable barracks by anyone's standards. Of course, we spent very little time in them.*

*RB15 capsize drills in the Gulf of Mexico. A refreshing, though salty, diversion.*

*The initial wave of the assault on our Ranger TACs. They didn't have a chance.*

*Our family portrait. I must admit, we were tempted to leave the TACs there for high tide.*

*In preparation for helicopter rappelling, we practiced on this tower. How I regretted not being able to rappel with my 'nerf' ruck.*

*The jungle. Not so formidable during the day, but at night...*

# CHAPTER 8

# OUT PROCESSING & GRADUATION

## 30 JULY 1980 (Out-processing: Day 58)

**Paperwork will ruin any military force.**
Lieutenant General Lewis B. 'Chesty' Puller
Quoted in Davis, MARINE, 1962

One more day! We spent the morning filling out forms and turning-in equipment at the Central Issue Facility (CIF). During the afternoon, we turned in weapons, conducted graduation rehearsal, and followed up with some more out-processing. Dinner was our final Super Supper. It was an excellent meal of steak, chicken, watermelon, and beer. We held it outside in the picnic area. Guests were invited and quite a few showed up. Overall, an excellent meal and time.

Nothing else was planned for the night. The cadets who did not pass are going into post. Feel badly for Mac.

Those who passed stay here. It is now 16 hours and counting. It's hard to believe that it is almost over. We started with 161 Rangers in our class. Tomorrow, there will be 90 Rangers standing on the field for graduation, with a number of them being recycles from other classes.

Once I am home, I am going to have to sit back and reflect on everything that transpired to understand what really happened out here. As of yet, there has been absolutely no time to contemplate this adventure.

SLEEP: 310001—310300 TOTAL: 3 Hours
Missed Meals: none

## 31 JULY 1980 (Graduation: Day 59)

**There are no secrets to success; don't waste time looking for them ... Success is the result of perfection, hard work, learning from failure, loyalty to those for whom you work and persistence. You must be ready for opportunity when it comes.**

General Colin Powell, quoted in
*The Washington Post*, 15 January 1989

Well ... it is finally here; the light at the end of the tunnel and no, it was not a mirror. The day that would never arrive. We were up early to clean the billets, eat, and move out. We performed details for three hours in the morning but most of us did a good job goldbricking. We rehearsed graduation for the last time and I collected my $20 bet from Mat for a steak dinner—no chew in this Ranger's mouth.

Finally, 1100 arrived. It was a good feeling having the USMA liaison officer pin on our 'blood' Tabs—a ritual by which the Tab is fastened to the sleeve of the uniform by a pin that punctures the skin of the arm beneath. There are quite a few guests here despite the 100+ degree temperature. A classmate's father was the guest speaker. After a running Pass in Review, we moved to the classroom where we quickly exchanged our PCs for a graduation certificate.

*****

**I am now history, and the proud owner of the Coveted Black and Gold.**

*****

# GRADUATION

*Super Supper. A fine meal in a relaxing atmosphere. The start of our acclimation and assimilation back into civilization.*

*There was a light at the end of the tunnel. Though fifteen pounds lighter (see first picture) and a wee bit tired, Cadet Lock is ready to head home with the Coveted, and hard-earned, Black and Gold proudly worn on his left shoulder.*

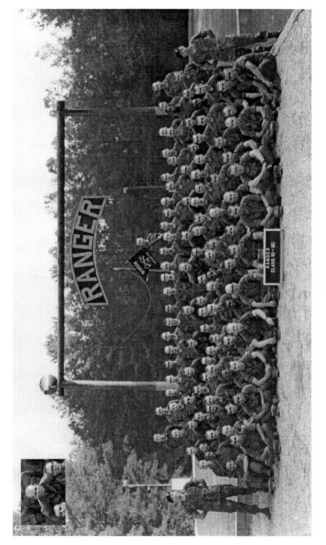

**Ranger Class 10-80**

*Ranger Class 10-80 Graduation picture. Note the sunken eyes. The author is located in the sixth row from the front, seventh from the left and seventh from the right...dead center.*

Be it known that

CADET JOHNNY D. LOCK

has successfully completed the

Ranger Course

at this institution and that in testimony

thereof is awarded this

# Diploma

Given at Fort Benning, Georgia, on this the

31ST day of    JULY,   nineteen hundred and EIGHTY

*Major General, USA*
Commandant

*Colonel, Secretary*

*Brigadier General, USA*
*Assistant Commandant*

*Ranger School Diploma with the author's awarded 'Coveted Black and Gold.'*

# CHAPTER 9

# THE PERILS OF RANGER TRAINING

We need to do realistic training, but good units don't kill their own people in combat, and they don't do it in training, either.

General Wayne Downing,
Commander SOCOM, 1995

To become a Ranger, a soldier must suffer to prepare him for what he may face on the field of battle. It is not a survival course, it is a test, an experience as close to real combat as possible. Ranger training is often dangerous and has been described as "about as close to terminal misery as the Army gets." That is as accurate a description of the course as any.

Unfortunately, simulating stressful, combat conditions can accidentally lead to tragedy. In the winter of 1977, two students died of hypothermia when they lost contact with their main element in the Florida swamp. In 1985, again while in the Florida phase, a soldier drowned while trying to cross a stream against a strong current. Other deaths during Ranger School, while not directly attributable to the course, per se, were no less tragic. While training during the Mountain Phase in March 1992, a student, unknown to the Ranger Cadre, carried the sickle cell anemia trait that proved to be fatal for him when placed at high altitude and under stress. Then, five months later, a Ranger fell to his death while negotiating the slide for life.

On 15 February 1995, the worst incident in the 44-year history of the school occurred when Ranger Class 3-95 entered the swamp for their first full day of training on day 9 of their 15 day Florida Phase. Scheduled as an introduction to the swamps of Florida, this introduction would prove to be a deadly experience for four of the class's Ranger students as the class crossed the deep running, tea-colored Yellow River later that evening.

The day's events began on the 15th at 0630, when the Ranger Camp battalion commander received a weather update at Eglin Air Force Base Auxiliary Field Six—50 miles east of Pensacola, Florida, otherwise known as Camp James E. Rudder: cloudy with a 30 percent chance of rain, highs in the 70s, lows in the 60s, wind from the south at 10 to 15 mph, water temperature of 50 degrees, water depth knee to upper thigh. Organized into three 34 student companies, Alpha, Bravo, and Charlie, the class of 102 students began its movement towards its insertion points by late morning and early afternoon. It was noted at this time that the water level had risen 12 to 18 inches. Based upon the air and water temperatures, the decision was made to continue with the swamp movement as planned.

At 1430, the C Company Ranger student patrol leader missed the designated landing site and was allowed by the RI to continue down river for another two kilometers. Water levels continued to rise another 3 to 5 inches. Reaching the landing site at 1519, B Company opted to move another several hundred meters from the site to cut their travel time in the water once they disembarked. Once at this location, though, they found that the water was too deep. C Company Rangers began to disembark at their location around 1600. At approximately the same time, A Company arrived at its drop-off site and found it too deep. The accompanying RI moved the unit to a dry insertion point on the debarkation side of the river where the company disembarked and moved 2 kilometers to a road. Following C Company to their drop site, B Company began to off-load at 1700.

As these events were unfolding, the Ranger battalion command remained unaware of the fact that the waters were rising rapidly. Soon after entering the water, one student from C Company and another from B Company began to display early signs of hypothermia, the lowering of the body's internal temperature below 95 degrees Fahrenheit—the consequence of losing body heat faster than it can be replaced—which resulted in an RI calling for an aerial MEDEVAC. Fatigued, stressed, weakened by lack of food, and weighing on average 10 to 20 percent less than they did when they started the course, the Rangers were rapidly losing body heat from the water faster than from the air.

By 1720, the water was so deep in the Crane Branch Creek, the vicinity of their landing, that the Rangers of B and C Companies were swimming to stay afloat in the Cypress and Cedar swamp with some of the students fighting to keep from being totally submerged. Blundering into water that was over their heads at times and beginning to collapse from exhaustion, B Company finally made the decision to build a one-rope bridge across the Crane Branch Creek.

Having arrived in the vicinity of Crane Branch Creek, the Ranger Battalion Commander began to assess the situation. By 1729, the Staff Duty NCO at Camp Rudder tripped the camp's siren in response to the MEDEVAC request.

For the next 45 minutes, C Company, located approximately 150 meters from B Company, struggled as students swam from tree to tree. Left with no other choice, this company also constructed a one-rope bridge to cross the Crane Branch Creek. Soon, another student began to show signs of hypothermia.

Meanwhile, the MEDEVAC of B Company's hypothermia took place from 1740 to 1835. Originally reported as one student, three Ranger students were evacuated to Camp Rudder's Troop Medical Clinic where they arrived at 1850. As a result of the quick response, these students survived the ordeal but, during the rescue, the beating blades of the helicopter disrupted voice communications thus causing three

Ranger students to drift away from the company. On their own, these three students moved out to higher ground and safety. As events were to show later, the hour of hovering by the MEDEVAC helicopter to find the unit would prove to be costly in terms of fuel consumption.

With the sun having set at 1827, B Company resumed its movement towards dry ground at 1840. Cold and cramping, the students found it difficult to move and, soon thereafter, the company began to fragment as the cold began taking its toll. Students began to lose and discard equipment, weapons, and the only operational unit radio, thus severing the company's communication with Camp Rudder.

Weather conditions continued to deteriorate as a dense fog began to move in. By 1900 hours, C Company had been in the water for their maximum emersion limit of three hours based upon the original estimate of 50–55 degrees. By 1920, the B Company RI had moved eight students to high ground and built a fire to help guide and warm the company.

The rescue effort began to significantly unravel by 1930 when B and C Companies requested another MEDEVAC only to find that the helicopter was out of fuel. Fuel was unavailable at Camp Rudder and a request had to be submitted to Eglin Air Force Base for a fuel truck. At this point in time, the Battalion Commander was under the mistaken impression that all was under control.

At 2000 hours, B Company reached its maximum immersion time. Forty-five minutes later, A Company, having completed its ambush training, learned of the severity of the situation and stood by to conduct rescue operations.

By 2100 hours, the battalion chain of command began to realize that something was horribly wrong. After hearing a Ranger student call for help or his Ranger Buddy would die, the battalion Command Sergeant Major, who was on site, began to gather all available RIs to assist with the rescue effort. Having been refueled, the MEDEVAC departed Camp Rudder for B Company's location in the swamp.

At 2115, the Battalion Commander, finally realized that the Ranger students were in a life or death situation and began to mobilize all of the Camp Rudder personnel to assist in search and rescue efforts to get the Ranger students out of the swamp and onto high ground.

By 2145 hours, the MEDEVAC was hovering over B Company's location but was having a great deal of difficulty spotting the location from which to make the extraction. Matters only became worse later as the stretcher with a Ranger on it became hung-up on a tree as it was being extracted. While attempting to maneuver the stretcher, the cable snapped, dropping the Ranger 10 to 20 feet back into the water. Eight minutes later, the helicopter was able to extract two students with a jungle penetrater but the helicopter's hovering over the unit's location exposed the remaining Rangers to additional cool temperatures from the rotor's backwash. Arriving at the hospital at 2050 hours, one student was pronounced dead at 0143 hours on the 16th. The second student recovered after being hospitalized for two days.

Grounded by limited visibility at Eglin, the MEDEVAC was unable to respond to C Company's call for assistance. Unable to evac the students by air, it took the C Company RIs nearly an hour to drag their two incapacitated students through the swamps to high ground, administering mouth-to-mouth resuscitation and cardiopulmonary resuscitation (CPR) along the way. Shivering students continued to shed weapons and equipment. Finally, the entire class was evacuated from the swamp and the exercise was canceled. Forced to transport the casualties by vehicle to two different hospitals at 2347 hours, the two students were pronounced dead on arrival around 0130 hours.

Just minutes after the ground evacuation of these two students took place, the cadre realized that they were missing a student. Continuing their search until 0230 hours, the Ranger cadre's search was finally called off by the Battalion Commander to prevent any additional deaths or injuries among the searchers. The search was resumed at 0530 and the last Ranger student's body was located in waste deep water just 75 meters from high ground. Transported to the hospital, he was pronounced dead at 0853 hours.

On 17 February, a memorial service was held at Camp Rudder for the four Rangers who died: Captain Milton Palmer, 27, The Citadel, Class of 1990; 2LT Spencer Dodge, 25, USMA 1994; 2LT Curt

Sansoucie, 23, USMA 1994; SGT Norman Tillman, 28, 1-325th Airborne Infantry Regiment, 82d Airborne Division. Having been awarded the Ranger Tab posthumously, the bodies of the deceased were escorted to their hometowns by representatives of the Ranger School.

On 24 February, the remaining 98 Rangers of Class 3-95 stood on a field at Fort Benning for the pinning of their Coveted Black and Gold Ranger Tabs. COL(Ret) Ralph Puckett was the graduation guest speaker. Commenting on why the good ones always go first, COL Puckett provided the following observations:

> The good ones go first because they are the good ones. They volunteer for the tough jobs. They want to be Rangers. They strive for excellence in everything they do. They push themselves. They know that "good enough" is never "good enough" until it's the best that they can do. They give 100 percent and then some to every job. Those young Rangers whom we lost were some of the best. They were some of the good ones. They gave their lives for their country as surely as if they had died on a battlefield in some far-flung corner of the world.
>
> Because of these deaths, there are people who would curtail Ranger training. There are those who say that we should never expose our best to risk. I disagree. Ranger training is the best close combat, small unit leadership and tactics training given in our Army. Ranger training is the best life insurance for the battlefield that we have. Ranger training will save more lives in combat than will ever be lost in training. If anyone has any doubts, he should ask a combat infantryman who had Ranger training before he heard the first shot fired. Ask any commander who has Ranger trained officers and non-commissioned officers under his command. Ask any Ranger graduate. The unanimous answer will be, "Ranger training is the best training I ever received!" Last week, the *Columbus Ledger-Enquirer*

quoted an old Ranger who said that Ranger training was the toughest thing he had ever endured. He said that but for the toughness he developed during Ranger training he would not have survived his two years as a POW during the Korean war!

Ranger training *is* the best training and any attempts to curtail its difficulty should be thwarted. But, while Ranger training is meant to be exceptionally tough, demanding, stressful, and realistic, students are not meant to die. Three investigations into the deaths were ordered: one by the Air Force because the deaths occurred on an Air Force installation, one by the Ranger Training Brigade Headquarters at Fort Benning, and one by the U.S. Army Safety Board, Fort Rucker, Alabama.

What went wrong? Deprivation of food and sleep, constant stress and evaluation, that is what Ranger School is all about. But Ranger training does not constitute real combat. No training, in peace or war, is worth the life or limb of a soldier. No amount of training can justify training deaths. Death is not an acceptable alternative, nor is needlessly endangering one's soldiers. Following this terrible tragedy, many articles and commentaries made note of how "Ranger training is the best" and "only a Ranger understands." While these statements are true, it does not give license to do foolish things and to risk lives.

The final investigative results indicated that a combination of events contributed to this disaster. Unfortunately, the vast majority of these events proved to be the result of human error. As determined by the investigations, the major contributors to this tragedy were an inadequate safety risk assessment and the failure to ensure adequate safeguards were in place. The combination of unexpected weather conditions led to an erroneous risk assessment. While the water temperature of 52 degrees was 2 degrees above the minimum 50 degree threshold set after the 1977 hypothermia deaths, the assessors failed to realize that prolonged exposure to chilled air of 60 or 65 degrees can bring on hypothermia; especially when these temperatures and exposure times are combined with the student's significantly fatigued state. The water depth was significantly underestimated and, even though the accompanying RIs were well aware of this factor, two of the three companies opted to continue with the original plan. As events began to unfold and the situation turned to confusion and then to chaos, the Rangers found themselves in the swamp for six hours, twice the time authorized, with the vast majority of the additional time a result of having to construct one-rope bridges and to MEDEVAC hypothermia victims.

From the start of the exercise that day, adequate safeguards were not in place, beginning with a general lack of experience among the instructors themselves. Allowing the boats to move farther into the swamp, the B and C Company instructors found themselves in deep water, strong currents, and unfamiliar territory. Communications proved to be woefully inadequate and no SOP existed for mass casualty evacuations. Even if a mass casualty evacuation SOP existed, the nearest medical facility, Camp Rudder, clearly had no ability to refuel the MEDEVAC helicopters.

The Army's report stated that there was a "failure in supervision and judgment, lack of situational awareness, and lack of control" for the accident. While nine RIs were disciplined, to include the relief of the Florida Phase Battalion Commander, none were court-martialed for there was found to be no basis for criminal charges.

Could this have been a case where the Ranger ethic went awry? Quite possibly. There is an adage that all Rangers have heard—and used themselves, "Ranger Tabs will keep you warm." It stimulates that drive-on attitude that enables a Ranger to persevere during tough times. The caveat to that perseverance, though, is that it also enforces a mentality that makes Ranger students reluctant to slow the pace or call attention to themselves even at the risk of their health.

The saddest fact about the exercise was that four Rangers died and nine careers were ruined for absolutely no reason. It did not have to happen. Some may call this Monday morning quarterbacking. I prefer to call it common sense. Adequate control measures had been in place prior to the arrival of the incumbent Battalion Commander. Winter training rules were established to keep students out of the water at night to decrease their overall exposure and to minimize the potential of becoming a hypothermia victim. For each of these swamp exercises, the Battalion Commander was the risk assessor who determined whether or not the conditions were too risky. Upon assuming command, the incumbent Battalion Commander scrapped that policy and delegated the responsibility down to the RI platoon instructor level with the belief that the field instructors were more knowledgeable and experienced than the camp staff. Unfortunately, that proved not to be the case in this situation for the primary instructor for this fatal mission had been in charge of the first day of swamp training only once before and had never walked the route taken by the students who died. Where was the knowledge? Where was the experience?

Students must have faith in their instructors and in the Army that their lives will not be needlessly endangered. The RIs placed their students in danger and then could not save them when they were overcome with exposure. Had some members of the chain-of-command and RIs not lost sight of their responsibilities by becoming trapped in the belief of their own invincibility, Ranger Class 3-95's initial baptism in the Cypress swamps of Florida would have just been another in the long line of miserable experiences Rangers endure.

With the completion of the investigations and the implementation of thirty-eight safety measures, Ranger School waterborne training in Florida resumed in the fall of 1995. New equipment is now on hand to assist troubled students; equipment which includes one-man inflatable rafts designed to get Rangers out of the water and to arrest hypothermia, water measuring devices, and global positioning systems. Monitoring stations have also been installed in swamp locations to provide better information on weather and water conditions. Command and control procedures now include the Ranger Battalion Commander who will make the final call as to whether waterborne operations are a Go, No Go, or modified—on-site RIs also have the authority to call off an operation should the situation warrant it. Additionally, training lanes will be walked by RIs prior to the exercise and there will be no deviation in the landing sites for the patrols.

**Every waking and sleeping moment, my nightmare is the fact that I will give an order that will cause countless num-**

bers of human beings to lose their lives. I don't want my troops to die. I don't want my troops to be maimed. It is an intensely personal, emotional thing for me. ...Any decision you have to make that involves the loss of human life is nothing you do lightly. I agonize over it. It's not purely a question of accomplishing the mission ... but it's a question of accomplishing the mission with a minimum loss of human life and within an effective time period.

General H. Norman Schwarzkopf,

5 February 1991

Interview in the *Washington Post*

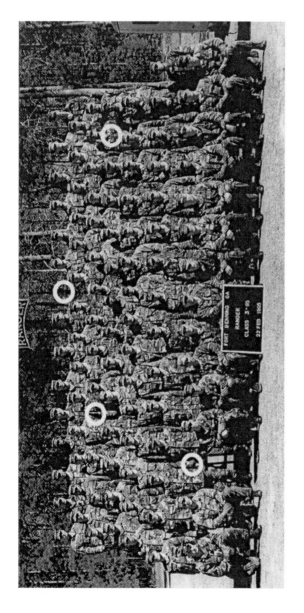

## Ranger Class 3-95

*Ranger Class 3-95 Graduation picture. Gaps were left in the formation in memory of their four lost comrades, Rangers Palmer, Dodge, Sansoucie, and Tillman. Note the symbolic ambulance to the right of the formation.*

# CHAPTER 10

# A RANGER'S DETERMINATION

## THE MAN IN THE ARENA

"It is not the critic who counts, not the man who points out how the strong man stumbled, or where the doer of deeds could have done better. The credit belongs to the man who is actually in the arena, whose face is marred by sweat and blood—who strives valiantly; who errs and comes short again and again, who knows the great enthusiasms, the great devotions, and spends himself in a worthy cause; who, at best, knows in the end the triumph of high achievement; and who, at the worst, if he fails, at least fails while daring greatly, so that his place shall never be with those cold and timid souls who know neither victory nor defeat."

Teddy Roosevelt

What is a Ranger? Colonel Puckett describes a Ranger as:

- a soldier with a special attitude—self assured, determined, demanding of himself and of those with whom he soldiers, a person for whom only his best is acceptable, a person who strives to be all that he can be.

- a product of hard, demanding, realistic training in a unit led by aggressive, motivated, example setting leaders who will not accept anything but the best. He has learned the most important lesson that anyone can ever learn and that is that there is no limit to what he can do; he can go just as far as his guts and brains will take him.

History is replete with the exploits of America's finest. Ranger commanders such as Robert Rogers, John Mosby, William Darby, and Bull Simons readily come to mind. Men of great deeds, exploits, and achievement. But are men such as these truly representative of what being a Ranger is all about?

In 1992, a man named Ed Caraccilo graduated from Rochester Institute of Technology. As a student, he volunteered to serve with the ROTC contingent at the school. Though he most assuredly would have received one, he didn't even apply for an ROTC scholarship; he just wanted to be a soldier.

After graduation, Ed was commissioned a second lieutenant in the Reserves. He attended the Infantry Officer Basic Course but because he did not solicit or receive an ROTC scholarship in school, he was not offered an active duty slot upon graduation from IOBC.

After trying for nearly four months to attain active duty status, 2LT Caraccilo wrote Colonel Grange, the commander of the 75th Ranger Regiment, requesting to be assigned to the 75th. Two weeks later, the Regimental Command Sergeant Major wrote back. Yes, Ed could be assigned to the 75th but it could not be as an officer. In that being an officer was not the issue, 2LT Caraccilo resigned his commission, reported to a local recruiter, and enlisted as an E4 with a Ranger contract.

Two months later, Ed reported to and graduated from the Ranger Indoctrination Program in December 1993 as the honor graduate of the course. Assigned to Alpha Company, 1st Battalion, 75th Ranger Regiment as a Karl Gustav assistant gunner, Specialist Caraccilo settled into his duties as a member of the Ranger Regiment. In the summer of

1994, after only seven months in the Battalion, Ed was selected to attend the Regiment's pre-Ranger course.

Upon completion of the pre-Ranger course and after entering Ranger School as part of class 11-94, Ed and nine other Rangers from the 1st Battalion passed the Benning Phase and moved on to the Desert. The Desert Phase, though, was not kind to these ten Rangers. Eight of the ten Rangers failed patrolling; an exceptionally high and abnormal rate considering the quality of soldiers involved. Unfortunately for Ed, he was one of the eight. Recycled, he went through the Desert Phase a second time…only to fail again. Fighting to recycle for a third time, Specialist Caraccilo was finally ordered back to his unit in October 1994.

Where most others would have said enough is enough, Ed borrowed a page from the Revolutionary War naval hero, Captain John Paul Jones—he had "only just begun to fight." He fought for and attained a second slot to attend the school. To so willingly and quickly endure this masochistic ritual a second time spoke volumes about his personal honor, character, and conviction.

In January 1995, he completed pre-Ranger for a second time. Entering with Ranger class 5-95, he endured the Desert Phase for a third time, the last class to go through that phase before its discontinuation. Finally, on 14 April 1995 on Malvesti Field, Specialist Caraccilo was presented the Merrill Marauders Award for his leadership and navigational skills along with his Coveted Black and Gold.

But, this Ranger's drive did not end there. Upon returning to 1st Batt and having the opportunity to go on a well deserved leave during which he could plan for his June wedding, Ranger Caraccilo opted to join his unit for Operation Ocean Venture in Puerto Rico, serving as a Ranger Team Leader in a weapons squad. Fortunately for him, his fiancée, Tracy, took care of the planning and the wedding went off without a hitch upon his return. She is obviously a Ranger's wife.

In July 1995, SPC Caraccilo took the OCS test and passed his boards in January 1996. Serving as acting AT Section Leader, Sergeant Caraccilo reported to OCS in May 1997. Commissioned in August of the same year, the second lieutenant reported to the 10th Mountain Division at Fort Drum where he spent two years serving as a rifle platoon leader, Scout platoon leader, and company executive officer in the 2-22 Infantry Battalion…the 'Triple Deuce.'

In July 1999, 1LT Caraccilo reported to ROP…Ranger Orientation Program…prior to being assigned to B Company, 2/75 Ranger Regiment in September to serve as a platoon leader. While most only fantasize of being able to obtain a lifetime dream, Ed was able to achieve his…having come full-circle to the point where he was able to lead those he once served with. I wish him, his wife, and three children the best of luck, though I honestly feel, luck will not be a factor in much that this Ranger does. To date, it never has.

Why do I hold Ranger Caraccilo's achievements in such high regards? Great accomplishments are expected of officers. For the most part, the service and the system train and groom them for success. However, tenacity, perseverance, and dedication as that displayed by Caraccilo is not expected from such junior soldiers. While officers plan, soldiers execute. Knowing that there are soldiers such as he who are members of the 75th Regiment leaves me secure with the knowledge that our Rangers will never fail. The creed is alive and well for it is inculcated in soldiers like Ranger Caraccilo.

> **William James, the noted American philosopher, would be proud of you. James said that we go through life without ever knowing the great potential, the great strength, we have deep down inside us. We never know because we are never sufficiently challenged; life is too easy. He said that war is the greatest challenge that man ever faces. It is in combat more than any other activity that man learns about that hidden strength, that hidden courage. James said that because combat is so destructive, we need a "moral equivalent of war." You have met your moral equivalent of war in Ranger training.**
>
> COL(Ret) Ralph Puckett, Jr., 24 February 1995
> Graduation Comments to Ranger Class 3-95

# CHAPTER 11

# FINAL THOUGHTS

During Ranger training, you have learned the most valuable lesson that anyone ever learns. You know that you can go just as far as your guts and your brains will take you. You've learned some other lessons. You know that after Ranger training, every day is a holiday and every meal is a banquet! You also know that you should never stand when you can sit, never sit when you can lie down, never stay awake when you can go to sleep, and never pass up the opportunity to get a bite to eat, take a drink of water, or go to the bathroom!

> COL(Ret) Ralph Puckett, Jr., 24 February 1995
> Graduation Comments to Ranger Class 3-95

Looking back over the daily entries of sleep and meals, one will find that I averaged three hours of sleep and two meals per day throughout the 59-day period. Quite obviously, this lack of sleep and food took its toll and recovery from this journey was a challenge in and of itself.

My first days home found me rotating between the bed, kitchen, and bathroom on a routine basis, and my family's food budget took a significant hit. For my first meal at home, I consumed 18 slices of

French toast for breakfast—only stopping at that number because my mother ran out of bread.

Physical recovery, especially in terms of body mass and endurance, took months to accomplish. There was one area, in particular, that took the greatest beating of all—my feet. Full feeling to these modes of conveyance did not return until Thanksgiving, nearly four months after graduation.

Ranger School is a great and lasting experience, an experience that you will always remember and talk about. Months after my graduation from Ranger School, I invited one of my sponsors, a Ranger qualified field grade officer, to a dining-in at West Point. At our table in the cadet mess, sat another senior officer, who was also Ranger qualified. Both men were infantrymen and each was a veteran of at least two combat tours in Vietnam. What I found most amazing was the fact that they spent the majority of the dinner telling each other war stories, not of Vietnam, but of Ranger School! When I asked them why they were discussing war stories of Ranger School rather than Vietnam, they stated that Ranger School was the more difficult of the two.

Now, not being a Vietnam Vet myself, I do not know whether to believe their claim that Ranger School was the more difficult of the two. I do believe, though, that it is safe to say that Ranger School will provide you a unique opportunity to learn things, both good and bad, about yourself and your classmates that will stay with you for a lifetime. The deprivations, adversity, exhaustion, and stress will quickly strip away any facade and reveal the true core of any man. In the process, it will assist your transformation into a warrior and leader of combat soldiers. It is an experience and accomplishment that no one can take from you.

Ranger School is just the beginning for those with the true warrior spirit. It is tough. It is difficult. It is excruciatingly demanding. It is "just a long continuous suck," exclaim graduates. In the end, it must be all these for today's modern...and unconventional battlefield...is even more unforgiving than those previously faced.

On the nation's behalf, Rangers are America's "killers"..."attack dogs for democracy"...trained to violate that most sacred of human sanctions...and one of God's Ten Commandments..."Thou shalt not kill." U.S. Army Rangers are America's premier direct-fire combat assault troops. A Ranger graduate is trained to enter the world's most dangerous neighborhoods, to fight face to face with the best, most unconventional fighters...and win. As the Battle of Bakara Market in Mogadishu on 3 October 1993 clearly demonstrated, those neighborhoods are festering swamps of unfettered, brutal, chaotic, uncivilized, no-quarter-given firefights. Only the most hardened and well trained have the best probability of surviving...physically as well as emotionally. In the end, Ranger School saves lives and achieves national, strategic goals.

In my introduction to this book, I mention "Ranger School is a structured series of events that earns one the right and privilege to be awarded the Ranger Tab, to be worn with pride on the left shoulder of a soldier's uniform." Unfortunately, there are those who believe that the earning of the Tab is an end in itself, another "check the block" item on the way to higher rank. As I was so rightly reminded by COL (Ret) Ralph Puckett in a letter to me, "the ultimate objective of Ranger School is a much more highly skilled close ground combat leader" who will "earn the Tab every day." The Coveted Black and Gold is not the "end" state for the professional soldier; it is the beginning!

In closing, this journal took on a life form of its own as I revised it. While this is only one man's story, I believe it speaks for itself in reference to the Ranger School experience. The only bit of advice I would offer is the following:

It is my opinion that the intent of the Ranger Course is to evaluate, not teach, leadership. The small unit tactics and associated stresses and deprivations are merely the vehicle by which the RIs evaluate one's leadership abilities. If you act forcefully, act aggressively, and take charge, there is a high degree of probability that you will pass. Make the Creed part of who you are and never lose sight of the Coveted Black and Gold. You can be part of this elite group, also, if you want it badly enough.

*GOOD LUCK, RANGER.*

# APPENDIX A:

## *RANGER CLASS 10-80 GRADUATES*

This list is comprised of those who originally started with class 10-80 on Day 1 and graduated.

### DEPARTMENT OF THE ARMY
### HEADQUARTERS UNITED STATES ARMY
### INFANTRY CENTER
#### Fort Benning, Georgia 31905

PERMANENT ORDERS 142-1                    30 July 1980

| NAME | RANK | NAME | RANK |
|------|------|------|------|
| ADAMS, LARRY W. | SSG | MAHONEY, JOHN J. | CDT |
| ALMANZA, ERNEST J. | CDT | MALTEO, RODRIGO E. | CDT |
| AVERY, WALTER L. | SP4 | MARKEL, DANIEL D. | PFC |
| BENNETT, CRAIG W. | SP4 | MARKEN, GLENN C. | PFC |
| BESCH, THOMAS M. | CDT | MATTSON, DUANE R. | SP4 |
| BREYFOGLE, MELVIN E. | SGT | MAYVILLE, WILLIAM C. | CDT |
| CARR, FRED C. | CDT | MERRIGAN, KEVIN G. | CDT |
| CASSINGHAM, JACK H. | CDT | MILLEN, RAYMOND A. | CDT |
| CONNOLLY, PHILIP G. | CDT | MILLER, CLIFF | CDT |
| CUMMINGS, TIMOTHY J. | CDT | MORGAN, GLENN E. | CDT |
| DOMENICK, JOHN B. | CDT | MOSHER, ALAN M. | CDT |
| ELVERUM, MARTIN A. | PFC | MOTEN, MATTHEW | CDT |
| FLEMING, ROBERT C. III | CDT | O'LEARY, BRIAN D. | CDT |
| FRANCIS, SCOTT A. | CDT | OWENS, SCOTT | PV2 |
| GARCIA, RAFAEL J. Sr | CDT | PERCHATSCH, GREGORY R. | CDT |
| GILLETT, DOUGLAS L. | SP4 | PETRILLI, CHRISTOPHER J. | PV2 |
| GLUMM, KENT M. | PFC | POPPER, ALFRED T. | SSG |
| GORSKY, ALEX | CDT | PRETHER, DONALD M. | SGT |
| GRIFFAW, TERRANCE L. | PFC | PUETT, JOSEPH F. III | CDT |
| GROW, ROBERT P. | CDT | RAKES, BOBBY N. | CDT |

| | | | |
|---|---|---|---|
| GUENTHER, PETER A. | SGT | RODRIGUEZ, RUFINO | CPL |
| GUERRERO, CARLOS P. | PFC | ROLLER, WILLIAM C. | CDT |
| HALVERSON, LARRY A. | SP4 | ROLLINSON, SAMUEL S. | CDT |
| HAYSLETT, MICHAEL K. | PFC | ROSSI, MARK M. | SGT |
| HOLTKAMP, GREGORY D. | CDT | RUSSO, RANDALL R. | CDT |
| HUDACEK, JOHN K. | SP4 | SHEPHERD, CRAIG L. | SGT |
| JENNETT, JEFFREY M. | SGT | SIMPSON, GEORGE G. Jr | SGT |
| JOHNSON, SAMUEL H. | CDT | STEER, DAVID N. | CDT |
| JONES, TERRENCE A. | CDT | STEINRAUF, ROBERT L. | CDT |
| KING, DARYL G. | PFC | TERHUNE, JEFFREY W. | CDT |
| KNOTTS, LESTER W. | CDT | THOMPSON, WAYNE | PV2 |
| KUTTRUFF, JOHN C. | CDT | TODD, DAVID P. | CDT |
| LABIER, PAUL R. | PFC | VANOUS, DONALD J. II | PV2 |
| LAFRANCE, RICHARD C. Jr | PFC | WARF, MACKIE D. | PFC |
| LEE, DUDLEY D. | SGT | WATSON, DOUGLAS I. | PFC |
| LOCK, JOHNNY D. | CDT | WRENN, ROBERT E. | CDT |

Announcement is made of the following award.

Award: Ranger Tab
Date(s) or period of service: 31 July 1980
Authority: Paragraph 5-28, AR 672-5-1
Reason: Completion of United States Army Ranger Training

FOR THE COMMANDER:

/s/
ROSE A. WALKER
2LT, AGC
Asst AG

\*\*\*\*\*

## LEGEND & BREAKDOWN OF CLASS 10-80 BY RANK:

| ABBREVIATION | RANK | TOTAL NUMBER OF GRADUATES BY RANK |
|---|---|---|
| PV2 | Private, Second Class | 4 |
| PFC | Private First Class | 12 |
| SP4 | Specialist Fourth Class | 6 |
| CPL | Corporal | 1 |
| SGT | Sergeant | 8 |
| SSG | Staff Sergeant | 2 |
| CDT | USMA Cadet | 39 |
| Original Class Graduates | | 72 |

# THE HISTORY OF THE RANGER TAB

**A Documented Study by Ranger Robert Black**

The author would like to personally thank Ranger Black, a well-published author in his own right, for providing this definitive study of the US Army Ranger Tab for publication in this work.

The Ranger Tab is a form of individual identification. It is a symbol of those who have explored the outer limits of the human spirit. To earn the Ranger Tab requires proving to others, but more importantly to yourself, that you can travel a hard path and master adversity. The Ranger Tab is a statement of a volunteer brotherhood who choose to test themselves beyond the body—to test themselves to that level of determination that is found only in an unshakable will to prevail. Rangers presently on active duty frequently refer to earning the Ranger Tab as a rite of passage.

The history of the individual Ranger Tab is inextricably tied with Ranger Unit Insignia. As with Ranger Unit Insignia, the Ranger Tab has been exposed to the error and confusion that occurs when historical accuracy is sacrificed on the altar of expedience.

The genesis of contemporary Ranger shoulder identification is the red, white and black Ranger scroll designed by Sergeant Anthony Rada of the 1st Ranger Battalion in 1942. During World War II, that insignia was not authorized by the Army. In 1943, the War Department authorized a diamond-shaped patch of blue background with yellow/gold letters and edging bearing the word RANGERS; this insignia did not find favor with the Rangers. By the end of World War II, all Ranger battalions were wearing the unauthorized Rada scroll. In 1947, the blue Ranger insignia was abolished by the Army.

The 8th Army Ranger Company was the first Ranger unit formed for the Korean War; it was a Table of Distribution unit given no authorized Ranger shoulder identification. On 29 September 1950, the Ranger Training Center (Airborne) 3349th ASU was established at Fort Benning, Georgia. On the same day, the 1st, 2nd, 3rd$^r$, and 4th Ranger Infantry Companies (Airborne) were activated. These were volunteers, regular army airborne qualified soldiers, who were primarily from the 82nd Airborne Division. By Army designation, these companies were the lineal descendants of the World War II Ranger battalions. The outline of the parachute and the designation RANGER was on the Issue guidons.

The Korean War Ranger course was built upon lessons learned in World War II and conducted under many hard masters including Edwin Walker, a former commander of the 1st Special Service Force, John Singlaub of the OSS, Francis Dawson of the 5th Ranger Battalion, and Arthur "Bull" Simon of the 6th Ranger Battalion. When the Korean War Rangers were formed, the Rada scroll was unauthorized and no approved Ranger shoulder identification was available. In October 1950, Col, Van Houten, Commanding Officer of the Ranger Training Center, visited the Pentagon and discussed Ranger insignia with a representative of Department of the Army G1. Col. Van Houten preferred a scroll similar to the Rada scroll and in the same colors, but his driving need was to have an insignia to award the men of the original graduating cycle on 13 November 1950. Department of the Army had a patch in production (possibly a yellow and black Airborne Tab) and felt it was better to build esprit around Ranger activities instead of units.

In order to have the Tab for the initial graduates of the Ranger Training Center, Col. Van Houten accepted a yellow and black Tab. DA approval was given on 3 November 1950, the birth date of the Ranger Tab, The first award of the Ranger Tab was made to the men of the 1st, 2nd, 3rd and 4th Ranger Infantry Companies (Airborne) on 13 November 1950, The requirement to earn the Tab by individual completion of the course of instruction and authorization for permanent award of the Tab was established. Ranger Training Center Memo 9 January 1951 reads: "All individuals successfully completing a six-week or longer cycle of Ranger training are authorized to wear the Ranger shoulder sleeve insignia even though they may be, for some reason, reassigned out of A numbered Ranger Infantry Company (Airborne)."

Soldiers of proficient units have pride in their units. As an individual recognition, the yellow (soon to be called gold) and black Ranger Tab did not reflect unit pride. Most Korean War Rangers opted to wear the Tab but also to wear an unauthorized red, white and black scroll shoulder insignia, with the words AIRBORNE RANGER and their Company number. The word "yellow" was dropped without change to the Tab. The black and gold Ranger Tab, identical to that of today, was worn in combat in Korea in 1950 and 1951. When the Korean War became stalled in trench warfare, infiltration and deep penetration operations were no longer in vogue. Like the Ranger Battalions of World War II, the Ranger Infantry Companies (Airborne) were inactivated.

The Korean War Ranger experience ended when the last Airborne Ranger Company folded its guidon on 1 December 1951. No Ranger units remained on active duty.

In September 1951, the Army, seeking to spread Ranger leadership through its ranks, established the Ranger Department of the United States Army Infantry School at Fort Benning, Georgia. Men from the Ranger Companies were involved in this. Events of the Korean War had outrun administration and Department of the Army had not published regulations regarding the Tab. The first mention of the Ranger Tab in Army Regulations is in Change 2 of AR 600-70, dated 23 January

1953. There the Ranger Tab is listed under "Badges." Eligibility requirements are stated as "Successful completion of Company Grade Ranger Courses," and award authority was established as the Commandant of the Infantry School.

On 10 August 1957, Field Manual 21-50, RANGER TRAINING was published by Headquarters Department of the Army. Appendix VI is the instructors' guide on Ranger History. The First Special Service Force, who are described as "like the Rangers," are given 13 lines but were not given the Ranger Tab. No mention was made of the 29th Ranger Battalion who has not been retroactively awarded the Ranger Tab or the 5307th Composite Unit (Provisional) Merrill's Marauders, who would be. The use of terms such as "like the Rangers" or "Ranger-type" began to creep into Army lexicon without regard to historical accuracy.

In the peacetime year of 1960, two events occurred which would change Ranger history.

The first was the placement of Ranger lineage and battle honors from World War II and Korea with 1st Special Forces. The second was the retroactive award of the Ranger Tab to men of the 5307th Composite Unit (Provisional), popularly known as "Merrill's Marauders." A change of Army organization affected Ranger lineage. In the late 1950s, the organization of combat units was shaped by the specter of the nuclear battlefield. Infantry divisions would feature battle groups instead of our traditional regiments. With the regimental concept abandoned, to preserve the honors accrued in past wars, the Army developed the Combat Arms Regimental System (CARS). Certain units were selected to have their battle honors retained and the honors of some units were consolidated. There were no Ranger units on active duty. Ranger honors did not fit with any of the CARS selected regiments. Special Forces was a popular concept at the time, so the battle honors of the Rangers and the WWII 1st Special Service Force went to 1st Special Forces, even though the history and concepts of organization and employment were not in common.

In early 1960, there was a change of the rules regarding the award of the Ranger Tab; this developed with a letter from the Infantry School to Continental Army Command (CONARC) at Ft. Monroe. This was followed by an 18 February 1960 endorsement from CONARC to the Adjutant General, Washington, D.C. The subject of both documents was PROPOSED CHANGE TO AR 600-70.

The Infantry School letter stated that Korean War references indicate individuals who successfully completed the course of instruction conducted by the Ranger Training Center and thereby qualified Rangers would be authorized to wear the Tab on a continuing basis. As far as the Infantry School could determine, Department of the Army authority was never implemented; this was not a correct statement. Paragraph 5 of the Infantry School Letter constitutes a major change in the history of the Tab. It reads as follows: "THE UNITED STATES ARMY INFANTRY SCHOOL ALSO BELIEVES THAT INDIVIDUALS WHO WERE AWARDED A COMBAT INFANTRYMAN BADGE WHILE SERVING WITH A RANGER BATTALION (1ST—6TH INCLUSIVE) OR MERRILLS MARAUDERS, THE 5307TH COMPOSITE UNIT (PROVISIONAL), SHOULD BE GRANTED AUTHORITY TO WEAR THE RANGER TAB."

The CONARC endorsement to the Adjutant General informs the AG that "it appears the intent was to permit wear of the Ranger Tab by those individuals who have successfully completed Ranger training, regardless of the dates of such training. In this connection, it is believed a change to AR 600-70, essentially as recommended by the U.S. Infantry School, would clarify the point."

In Paragraph 2, CONARC agreed that the authority for wearing of the Ranger Tab should be extended "to include those individuals who were awarded the Combat Infantry Badge while serving with a Ranger Battalion or with Merrill's Marauders. These individuals, in some instances, may not have completed the prescribed Ranger training course but certainly have earned the right to wear the Tab by actual performance under combat conditions."

None of the language used later to justify the retroactive award of the Ranger Tab to WWII veterans and deny it to the LRRP and Vietnam Rangers was present in the Infantry School letter or the CONARC endorsement to the AG. These words include: "unique experience, intensive training and the specialized employment of these soldiers at a time when no formal school or special skill Ranger Tab had been established."

The Ranger Department and the Infantry School could have held the line. They could have reasoned that from the time of its inception authority to wear the Ranger Tab had been based on completion of the Ranger Training Course. The Ranger Infantry Companies (Airborne) of the Korean War met these requirements. The graduates of Ranger instruction that followed met these requirements. The men of World War II did not. They should not have been awarded the Tab, unless the intent was to grant it to others of World War II and later wars who were equally deserving but did not meet the Ranger course requirements.

Compare the retroactive award of the Ranger Tab to the Combat Infantry Badge. World War I Infantry veterans of the trenches were alive in 1960. The men of World War I, or men who fought in the infantry in wars prior to World War II, were not retroactively awarded the Combat Infantry Badge, though they clearly earned it.

Past President Ranger James Altieri of the Ranger Battalions Association of World War II wrote the author that their association did not request the retroactive award of the Tab. The Rangers of World War II thought of the Tab as a school patch and in Altieri's words "never thought the need to embellish ourselves with their patch." There is no indication or belief that the Merrill's Marauders Association as an association was behind this action, though they benefited from it. That this was arbitrarily "given to them" is provable by the exception of other WWII units who were equally or more entitled to the retroactive award of the Tab.

The United States Army never named nor gave indication that it considered the 5307th Composite Unit (Provisional) a Ranger unit during the existence of the unit. The 475th Infantry Regiment, with which the 5307th was consolidated on 10 August of 1944, was not named a Ranger unit, nor in 1960 was the 75th Infantry Regiment, which had absorbed the lineage of the 475th.

The 5307th Composite Unit (Provisional) was organized and had training to serve with the British in Burma as a Long Range Penetration

Group, a British term used for empire forces under Orde Wingate. The 5307th did not fight with Wingate's men as a deep penetration unit, but served under General Stilwell in envelopment tactics. Stilwell used two Chinese Divisions to attack the Japanese 18th Division in the front while he enveloped their positions with the American 5307th C.P.U. and used OSS detachment 101, leading thousands of Kachin guerrillas in the Japanese rear. Stilwell called his use of the 5307th "an end run." The copy of the draft of the history of the 5307th submitted to Merrill and Stilwell for their personal review shows that in describing the 5307th operations, these commanders lined out the draft description of "modified form of Long Range Penetration operations." They would not have done that if they considered the 5307th a Long Range Penetration Unit. Col. Hunter, a commander of the 5307th, on page 27 of his book "Galahad" confirms the method of employment in the end run (envelopment) sense.

The 1957 version of FM 21—50 Ranger training made no mention of the 5307th, yet in 1960 they were singled out over the First Special Service Force and the 29th Ranger Battalion for retroactive award of the Ranger Tab.

Of all the World War II Ranger Battalions, the 29th Provisional Ranger Battalion best reflects the philosophy and practice of the Ranger Course since late 1951. The 29th Ranger Battalion was formed by the European Theater command after the 1st Ranger Battalion departed England for North Africa. Comprised of volunteers from the 29th Infantry Division, these men underwent two months of preparatory training, then trained under the British Commandos for five weeks. Its members then participated in operations on the Norwegian coast with Lord Lovat's No.4 Commando. The 29th Infantry Division was scheduled to play a key role in the invasion of Europe and its commander wanted his men back. When the Ranger unit was disbanded, its members returned to the 29th Infantry Division and raised the level of small unit efficiency. On 6 June 1944 in the invasion of Normandy, the 2nd and 5th Ranger Battalions were attached to the 116th Infantry Regiment of the 29th Infantry Division. Men of the 29th Rangers were on the same beach, behind the same wall, and participated in the action that gave

Rangers the motto "RANGERS LEAD THE WAY." They then fought through to the heart of Nazi Germany, and the 2nd and 5th Ranger Battalions were again attached to the 29th Division in significant operations.

If "Ranger-type" or "units like the Rangers" were to be retroactively awarded the Tab, why wasn't the First Special Service Force included? This unique unit comprised of Americans and Canadians was given airborne, mountaineering and ski training. They had unique weapons and vehicles specially designed to move on snow. They were intended for use against the Germans in Norway. That did not come to pass and the Forcemen fought through the mountains of Italy to Rome, frequently using their special talents to attack German positions by climbing cliffs the Germans thought too steep to climb.

The result of this arbitrary selection was 1961 Army Regulations granting retroactive award of the Ranger Tab to any person awarded the CIB while serving as a member of Ranger Battalion 1st–6th, inclusive, or the 5307th Composite Unit (Provisional) (Merrill's Marauders), or to any person who completed a Ranger course conducted by the Ranger Training Command.

In January of 1962, Department of the Army published FM 21-50 RANGER TRAINING AND RANGER OPERATIONS. Appendix 17 of the manual is titled "Ranger History." Once again, these words were "the guide" for instructors. It begins with the usual error that Robert Rogers organized the Rangers. The First Special Service Force that was included in the 1957 manual is out and the 5307th described as a "Ranger-type" unit is in, with its combat exploits described in detail.

War in Vietnam brought a new set of challenges and the introduction of the Long Range Reconnaissance Patrol concept. In some staff papers refusing the retroactive award of the Ranger Tab to the men of Vietnam, it was argued that they were not Rangers because they operated in small groups. Those who take this position are not knowledgeable of Ranger history. Ranger units have performed many tasks, but all of us stem from the blend of European weapons and discipline and the

American Indian tactic of small bodies of men executing reconnaissance, ambush, and raid.

As the war in Vietnam was heating up, the men of the Merrill's Marauders Association were waging a valiant veteran's battle to gain approval of the patch they had designed while in combat. There is a voluminous file at the U.S. Army Military History Institute with documents from 1960 to 1968 that covers this struggle. The Marauders were fighting for historical correctness and fighting with the vigor of men who know an injustice has been done. This fight had nothing to do with anything "Ranger." They wanted their self-designed insignia from the days of their combat to be approved by the Army.

The 75th Infantry Regiment, which had been on Okinawa, was inactivated in 1957. The Merrill's Marauders Association also wanted the regimental colors with their combat streamers and their regiment on active service. They employed significant congressional pressure including Bobby Kennedy, Mendal Rivers, and other powers of the time. They kept the Department of the Army well aware of their existence. At this time, there is no indication that the men of this association thought of themselves as Rangers.

In the fall of 1968, several events occurred that are so close in timing that it is unlikely they are unrelated. By letter of 6 August 1968, the Department of the Army, Office of the Adjutant General, forwarded Ranger Tabs to Mr. Hurwitt, the Secretary of the Merrill's Marauders Association for distribution. Around this same time, a series of letters were being exchanged between Mr. Hurwitt, Secretary of the Merrill's Marauders Association, Colonel Charles Hunter also of the Association, and Lieutenant Colonel Bryan Sutton of the Office of the Assistant Chief of Staff for Force Development in Washington, D.C.

Sutton is described by those who knew him as a bright, dedicated staff officer; he was not a Ranger. In his correspondence, Sutton wrote that Department of the Army staff were considering redesignating Long Range Patrol units in Vietnam using Korean War Ranger Company Designations. Sutton was the action officer.

Sutton went to the Center for Military History, looking for a regimental home for the Rangers of Vietnam. He writes, and I quote:

"A check was made to determine which units in World War II conducted Special Mission operations. Three units came to light: The Ranger Battalions, 1st Special Service Force, and the 5307th Provisional Group (Merrill's Marauders). The Ranger Battalions and the 1st SSF were eliminated because their history is now part of the 1st Special Force. This then is how the 75th Infantry was selected to be the parent Regiment for our LRP units."

As example of the new arrangement, Co D (LRP) 17th Inf would become Co A (RANGER) 75th Infantry. The search for historical lineage that was to be based on World War II Ranger Battalions and Korean War Ranger Companies became one not of Ranger but "special mission" units.

As the intent was to designate the LRP units of Vietnam as Rangers, why didn't the Army in 1968 withdraw the honors of the World War II and Korean War Rangers from 1st Special Forces and create a Combat Arms Regimental System, Ranger Infantry Regiment, as they did with 1st Special Forces? There would then have been an accurate Ranger honors trace going: Ranger Battalions of World War II—Ranger Companies of Korea—Ranger Companies of Vietnam.

The Combat Arms Regimental System had been approved at the Secretary of the Army level. It requires the same level of approval to make a change. According to the Center for Military History, the Army policy is "once given, honors are not withdrawn." This is a policy that is detrimental to truth. In order not to disrupt CARS, historical accuracy went by the wayside. We will never know if they could have gotten Secretary of the Army approval to give Ranger units an accurate historical trace. The point is...in 1968, they didn't try.

The second paragraph of a letter from Colonel Hunter of the Marauders Association to Lieutenant Colonel Sutton dated 15 October 1968 contains the following words: "As you know, the Merrill's Marauders Association has been attempting to secure its approval of its recognized patch without success. The approval of the Ranger Tab is considered a SOP and not satisfactory..." Hunter's consideration of the Tab can be read as SOP, which is something given as a reward, concession or appeasement, a bribe, or as the abbreviation of Standard

Operating Procedure, which doesn't fit. Either way, a low regard for the Ranger Tab by this former commander of the 5307th is clear.

Sutton's 1 November 1968 memo sought Chief of Staff of the Army approval to activate the 75th Infantry as the parent organization for all DA authorized LRP units and to redesignate them as Ranger. Sutton wrote that "...redesignating LRP's using the Korean War Ranger Company designations is not feasible without disrupting CARS." Again, historical accuracy gave way before a concern for administrative procedures.

He wrote that the use of the term Ranger would "provide a strong appeal for recruiting more soldiers into the Ranger Training Program..." In later years, these words were revised to read that it was done to encourage men of LRP/Ranger units in Vietnam to attend the Ranger school at Fort Benning.

The great majority of the men who fought as Rangers in Vietnam volunteered while overseas. There is no reason to believe that if the Ranger Course had existed in World War II, the men of the 1st, 3rd and 4th Ranger Battalions (Darby's Rangers) or the 6th Ranger Battalion would have been sent home from England or North Africa or the Pacific to take the Ranger course before going into combat. There is no valid basis to believe that because a man earned the CIB while a member of Ranger Battalions 1-6, or the 5307th Composite Unit (Provisional) Merrill's Marauders, that he would have completed the Ranger Course of instruction. Numbers of these men were on active duty in the 1950s. Few took the opportunity to do the course, yet all were retroactively awarded the Tab.

The United States Army has never taken infantry units engaged in combat overseas, returned them to the United States for training, then sent them back to the same theater of battle. There were no programs to bring LRP/Ranger volunteers in Vietnam back to Fort Benning to allow them to complete the Ranger course before commitment to battle. These volunteers in Vietnam had no more chance to attend the Ranger course at Fort Benning than did the men of World War II. There is no indication that all the men who wanted to go to Vietnam to fight as Rangers were given a quota to attend the Ranger Course.

The Ranger Department was concerned that the LRPs not be given the Ranger Tab as was done with the 5307th. Paragraph 7 of Sutton's memo satisfies the Ranger Department objections with the words: "It will not degrade the graduates of the Ranger School since they will remain the only personnel to wear the Ranger Tab."

One day in Vietnam, a Long Range Patrol volunteer was waiting for a helicopter to take him and a few others off to the unique experience and specialized mission of staking out some distant trail in a reconnaissance or ambush mode. Several days later, the same man did the same mission, but now by direction of Department of the Army that same man was a Ranger serving in a Ranger unit—he was a volunteer. His officers were frequently Ranger School graduates who had the knowledge and experience to pass on the Ranger school doctrine. The non-commissioned officers who trained him were fresh from the battlefield experience giving him the latest information. His own experience was in the ultimate school of battle. Why should he not have Ranger pride? If Department of the Army says this same man who was Long Range Patrol is now Ranger, why should he not have some authorized form of Ranger shoulder identification?

He did not get it.

That which the Korean War Ranger earned and the World War II Ranger Battalions 1–6 and the 5307th were retroactively awarded was not granted to the LRP/Rangers of Vietnam. The DA implementing message stated they were not authorized to wear the Ranger Tab unless they had been awarded the Tab through successful completion of the U.S. Army Ranger Course at Ft. Benning, GA. The DA implementing message further stated, "personnel of the 75th Inf will wear the patch of the division or separate brigade to which they are attached. In a case of corps or Field Force companies, the Corps or Field Force patch will be worn."

There were substantial differences between the LRP/Ranger and the man in a rifle company of Vietnam. The LRRP/Ranger was a volunteer. He received specialized training; his mission was unique. The Department of the Army had declared him a "Ranger." As he was a Department of the Army designated Ranger, it is reasonable that he should have an authorized unit or individual shoulder identification with the word Ranger thereon.

Some 373 of these men were killed in action, died of wounds or were missing in action and not returned. DA General Orders Number 7 dated 14 February 1986 informs that the 75th Ranger Regiment (Merrill's Marauders) is credited with 17 campaigns from Vietnam. The colors of the Regiment are authorized one Presidential Unit Citation streamer, six Valorous Unit award streamers, and three meritorious Unit Commendation streamers, all from Vietnam. But the men who earned the honors of Vietnam have nothing authorized to wear that says "Ranger."

The close of the war in Vietnam brought, as it has for all of us who preceded them, the inactivation of their Ranger units. January of 1974 saw the activation of the 1st Battalion (Ranger) of the 75th Infantry, and October of that year brought the activation of the 2nd Battalion. But these Ranger Battalions did not carry the history and battle honors of the World War II Ranger Battalions and the Ranger Companies of Korea. The battle honors the World War II and Korean War Rangers had fought for was with the 1st Special Forces and the Ranger regiment that historically should have carried our lineage had been given to the 5307th CPU (Merrill's Marauders).

In the early 1980s, the formation of the Korean War Ranger Association and the establishment of a close bond with the Rangers Battalion Association of World War II had a profound effect. As civilians, we could attack historical inaccuracies of insignia and lineage. The formation of the Ranger Regiment and selection of Wayne Downing, a man who cared about Ranger history, as its commander was critical. Grenada was a magnificent triumph for the Rangers. They jumped wearing the Rada scroll and, 41 years after its birth, it became an authorized insignia. Once again, Rangers were in the public eye.

Then began a battle that pitted World War II and Korean War Rangers against those tied to the 75th lineage with Secretary Marsh between the lines of fire. The Rangers of World War II and Korean War Rangers wanted the Ranger Regiment to have the heritage that we knew we established. We wanted this first Ranger infantry regiment in our nation's history to be named the 1st Ranger Regiment. We wanted what we knew to be clearly an accurate "Ranger" lineage.

What had happened was not the fault of the Merrill's Marauders Association. They had fought for their rightful historical recognition. They wanted an insignia they had designed and were proud of; they wanted their colors and honors and their regiment on active service. Theirs was not a fight to be called Ranger. Through lack of definition, unwillingness to disrupt CARS, and historical error, by people on active duty and at the Center of Military History, the Ranger Tab and the Ranger Regiment fell their way.

The Rangers of World War II and Korea did not win the fight to have the first Ranger regiment so named. Past error had created a no-win situation. The Ranger honors of Vietnam and Grenada were with the 75th. What they would not do in 1968 when they could have had accuracy, the Department of the Army did in 1986. They withdrew World War II Ranger Battalion and Korean War Ranger Company honors from 1st Special Forces and incorporated them into the 75th Ranger Regiment (Merrill's Marauders). Eighteen campaigns were added to the two from the 5307th CPU (Merrill's Marauders) and the seventeen from Vietnam.

By letter dated September 24, 1985, DA authorization was granted for the retroactive award of the Ranger Tab to those CIB winners of the Korean War, 8th Army Ranger Company.

This report on history of the Ranger Tab is documented and files complete with documentation were provided the Infantry Center Library and key personnel at the Ranger Regiment and Ranger Training Brigade. The veterans who made our traditions did not generate what has happened. It was a self-inflicted wound generated at Fort Benning and at Department of the Army, who in the 1960s were careless with historical fact.

In 1997, a board convened at Fort Benning reaffirmed that the Ranger Tab would not be retroactively granted to the Rangers of Vietnam as it was done for the men of World War II. Precedent, historical fact, and documentation proved no impediment to a forgone conclusion and economy of the truth ruled. The truth is that the Ranger Tab will not be granted to the men of Vietnam as it would mean that all men who engage in future combat as Rangers would have a claim to the Tab.

The board drafted a recommendation seeking retroactive approval for the Rangers of Vietnam to wear the insignia of the 75th Ranger Regiment. There are no indications that a follow-through effort was made to bring this to pass. The Rangers of Vietnam are still the only members of the Ranger family who are not authorized something that says "Ranger."

The criteria for earning the award of the Tab have remained essentially unchanged in Army regulations from 1961 to the present. Completion of the Ranger Course is a requirement.

The problems of the Ranger Tab and indeed Ranger history is in large part caused by the lack of a clear-cut definition of who is a Ranger. The Ranger Department, the Infantry School, and Department of the Army have in the past carelessly accepted the definition of a Ranger unit to include the use of terms "Ranger-type" and "Units like Rangers," and "Special Mission Units."

In his book *Raiders or Elite Infantry*, David Hogan of the Center for Military History writes that "By the time of the formation of LRRP units..., Ranger had become a term of legendary connotations but no precise meaning." For the want of a definition of who and what is a Ranger, integrity was lost.

As a result of Grenada, circumstances have changed. Since 1983, men have had the opportunity to earn and wear an authorized Ranger unit scroll or an authorized Ranger Tab or both. But there is a need for a firm definition of who and what constitutes a RANGER. Without that definition, we face the likelihood of future controversy.

> Ranger Robert Black rose through the ranks from Recruit to Colonel. He has been twice awarded the Combat Infantry Badge and holds the Silver Star and two Bronze Stars for Valor. He was the founding president of the Korean War Ranger Association and has written extensively on

Ranger activities from the 1600's to the present. He is the author of the books RANGERS IN KOREA and RANGERS IN WORLD WAR II. In 1995 he was inducted into the U .S. Army Ranger Hall of Fame.

# APPENDIX C:

# THE 'TRUTH' BEHIND ROGERS' RANGERS 'STANDING ORDERS'

The Ranger Handbook, SH 21-76, published by the Ranger Training Brigade of the United States Army Infantry School, states the following, in part, in regards to the Standing Orders of Rogers' Rangers: "Ranger techniques and methods were an inherent characteristic of the frontiersmen in the colonies, but Major Rogers was the first to capitalize on them and incorporate them into a permanently organized fighting force. His 'Standing Orders' were written in the year 1759. Even though they are over 200 years old, they apply just as well to Ranger operations conducted on today's battlefield as they did to the operations conducted by Rogers and his men." There are three sentences in that quote. The first is true, the second is false, and the third, based on the second, is inherently misleading.

On 14 September 1757, Rogers' "Ranging School" was officially authorized. Its first group of students were British Cadet volunteers. To structure his training, Rogers drafted twenty-eight tactical rules which came to be known as "Rogers' Rules of Discipline." In 1765, he would have them published as part of his French and Indian War Journals. His rules, as written, were detailed, comprehensive, and exceptionally insightful for the period. They proved to be so insightful, as a matter of fact, that they are still very much applicable to today's modern battlefield. The "Rules of Discipline" were truly a brilliant discourse on unconventional scouting and skirmishing and a very sound argument could be made that they constitute the first military field manual written on the North American continent.

So, then, where did the more succinct and entertaining "Roger's Standing Orders" come from? It just so happens that Robert Rogers served as the role model for Kenneth Roberts' protagonist in the 1936 novel *Northwest Passage*. Within the written conversation between the fictitious characters Langdon Towne and Sergeant McNott, in which McNott is explaining to Towne what a Ranger must know, one can find the foundation for the wording of what were to become the "Standing Orders." There should be no doubt that Kenneth Roberts' fictional conversation was predicated on Robert Rogers' Rules of Discipline.

This passage from the novel apparently struck a cord with an officer assigned to The Infantry School as a doctrine writer for the 1960 version of Field Manual (FM) 21-50, *Ranger Training and Ranger Operations*. Within this FM was an appendix on Ranger history that included a paraphrased version of the novel's passage attributed to Rogers and titled "Standing Orders." A year or two later, a review of the reprinted *Journals of Major Robert Rogers* by The Infantry School led the staff to question the validity of "Roger's Standing Orders." Despite an attempt on the part of the school to clarify the record, their efforts proved fruitless. Rogers' Standing Orders had become part of lore and legend.

The author is indebted to Major William H. Burgess III in regards to background on the questionable history of Roger's Standing Orders. In an article titled *The Real Rules of Discipline of Major Robert Rogers and the Rangers* printed in the July–August 1993 edition of *Infantry* Magazine, Burgess wrote of the discrepancy between the Rules of Discipline and the Standing Orders.

# APPENDIX D:

# ROGERS' RULES OF DISCIPLINE

*I.*     All Rangers are to be subject to the rules and articles of war; to appear at roll-call every evening on their own parade ground, each equipped with a firelock, 60 rounds of powder and ball, and a hatchet, at which time an officer from each company is to inspect them to see that they are in order, so as to be ready to march at a minute's warning; and before they are dismissed the necessary guards are to be chosen, and scouts for the next day appointed.

*II.*     Whenever you are ordered out to the enemy's forts or frontiers for discoveries, if your number is small, march in single file, keeping far enough apart to prevent one shot from killing two men, sending one man or more forward, and the like on each side, at a distance of 20 yards from the main body, if the ground you march on allows it, to give the signal to the officer of the approach of an enemy, and of their number, etc.

*III.*     If you march over marshes or soft ground, change your position and march abreast of each other to prevent the enemy from tracking you (as they would do if you marched in single file) until you get over such ground, and then resume your former order and march until it is quite dark before you encamp. Camp, if possible, on a piece of ground that gives your sentries the advantage of seeing or hearing the enemy at considerable distance, keeping half of your whole party awake alternately through the night.

*IV.*      Some time before you come to the place you would reconnoiter, make a stand and send one or two men in whom you can confide to seek out the best ground for making your observations.

*V.*      If you have the good fortune to take any prisoners, keep them separate until they are examined, and return by a route other than the one you used going out so that you may discover any enemy party in your rear and have an opportunity, if their strength is superior to yours, to alter your course or disperse, as circumstances may require.

*VI.*      If you march in a large body of 300 or 400 with a plan to attack the enemy, divide your party into three columns, each headed by an officer. Let these columns march in single file, the columns to the right and left keeping 20 yards or more from the center column, if the terrain allows it. Let proper guards be kept in the front and rear and suitable flanking parties at a distance, as directed before, with orders to halt on all high ground to view the surrounding ground to prevent ambush and to notify of the approach or retreat of the enemy, so that proper dispositions may be made for attacking, defending, etc. And if the enemy approaches in your front on level ground, form a front of your three columns or main body with the advanced guard, keeping out your flanking parties as if you were marching under the command of trusty officers, to prevent the enemy from pressing hard on either of your wings or surrounding you, which is the usual method of savages if their number will allow it, and be careful likewise to support and strengthen your rear guard.

*VII.*     If you receive fire from enemy forces, fall or squat down until it is over, then rise and fire at them. If their main body is equal to yours, extend yourselves occasionally; but if they are superior, be careful to support and strengthen your flanking parties to make them equal with the enemy, so that if possible you may repulse them to their main body. In doing so, push upon them with the greatest resolve, with equal force in each flank and in the center, observing to keep at a due distance from each other, and advance from tree to tree, with one half of the part ten or twelve yards in front of the other. If the enemy pushes upon you, let your front rank fire and fall down, and then let your rear rank advance through them and do the same, by which time those who were in front will be ready to fire again, and repeat the same alternately, as occasion requires. By this means you will keep up such a constant fire that the enemy will not be able to break your order easily or gain your ground.

*VIII.*     If you force the enemy to retreat, be careful in pursuing them to keep out your flanking parties and prevent them from gaining high ground, in which case they may be able to rally and repulse you in their turn.

*IX.*     If you must retreat, let the front of your whole party fire and fall back until the rear has done the same, heading for the best ground you can. By this means you will force the enemy to pursue you, if they pursue you at all, in the face of constant fire.

*X.*     If the enemy is so superior that you are in danger of being surrounded, let the whole body disperse and every one take a different road to the place of rendezvous appointed for that evening. Every morning the rendezvous point must be altered and fixed for the evening in order to bring the whole part, or as many of them as possible, together after any separation that may occur in the day. But if you should actually be surrounded, form yourselves into a square or, in the woods, a circle is best; and if possible make a stand until darkness favors your escape.

XI.     If your rear is attacked, the main body and flanks must face about the right or left, as required, and form themselves to oppose the enemy as directed earlier. The same method must be observed if attacked in either of your flanks, by which means you will always make a rear guard of one of your flank guards.

XII.    If you determine to rally after a retreat in order to make a fresh stand against the enemy, by all means try to do it on the highest ground you come upon, which will give you the advantage and enable you to repulse superior numbers.

XIII.   In general, when pushed upon by the enemy, reserve your fire until they approach very near, which will then cause them the greater surprise and consternation and give you an opportunity to rush upon them with your hatchets and cutlasses to greater advantage.

XIV.    When you encamp at night, fix your sentries so they will not be relieved from the main body until morning, profound secrecy and silence being often of the most importance in these cases. Each sentry, therefore, should consist of six men, two of whom must be constantly alert, and when relieved by their fellows, it should be without noise. In case those on duty see or hear anything that alarms them, they are not to speak. One of them is to retreat silently and advise the commanding officer so that proper dispositions can be made. All occasional sentries should be fixed in a like manner.

XV.     At first light, awake your whole detachment. This is the time when the savages choose to fall upon their enemies, and you should be ready to receive them.

XVI.    If the enemy is discovered by your detachments in the morning, and if their numbers are superior to yours and a victory doubtful, you should not attack them until the evening. Then they will not know your numbers and if you are repulsed your retreat will be aided by the darkness of the night.

XVII.    Before you leave your encampment, send out small parties to scout around it to see if there are any signs of an enemy force that may have been near you during the night.

XVIII.   When you stop for rest, choose some spring or rivulet if you can, and dispose your party so as not to be surprised, posting proper guards and sentries at a due distance, and let a small party watch the path you used coming in, in case the enemy is pursuing.

XIX.     If you have to cross rivers on your return, avoid the usual fords as much as possible, in case the enemy has discovered them and is there expecting you.

XX.      If you have to pass by lakes, keep at some distance from the edge of the water, so that, in case of an ambush or attack from the enemy, your retreat will not be cut off.

XXI.     If the enemy forces pursue your rear, circle around until you come to your own tracks and form an ambush there to receive them and give them the first fire.

XXII.    When you return from a patrol and come near our forts, avoid the usual roads and avenues to it; the enemy may have preceded you and laid an ambush to receive you when you are almost exhausted with fatigue.

XXIII.   When you pursue any party that has been near our forts or encampments, do not follow directly in their tracks, lest you be discovered by their rear guards who, at such a time, would be most alert. But endeavor, by a different route, to intercept and meet them in some narrow pass, or lie in ambush to receive them when and where they least expect it.

XXIV.    If you are to embark in canoes, or otherwise, by water, choose the evening for the time of your embarkation, as you will then have the whole night before you to pass undiscovered by any enemy parties on hills or other places that command a view of the lake or river.

XXV.      In paddling or rowing, order that the boat or canoe next to the last one wait for it, and that each wait for the one behind it to prevent separation and so that you will be ready to help each other in any emergency.

XXVI.      Appoint one man in each boat to look out for fires on the adjacent shores, from the number and size of which you may form some idea of the number that kindled them and whether you can attack them or not.

XXVII.      If you find the enemy encamped near the banks of a river or lake that you think they will try to cross for their security when attacked, leave a detachment of your party on the opposite shore to receive them. With the remainder, you can surprise them, having them between you and the water.

XXVIII.      If you cannot satisfy yourself as to the enemy's number and strength from their fires and the like, conceal your boats at some distance and ascertain their number by a patrol when they embark or march in the morning, marking the course they steer, when you may pursue, ambush, and attack them, or let them pass, as prudence directs you. In general, however, so that you may not be discovered at a great distance by the enemy on the lakes and rivers, it is safest to hide with your boats and party concealed all day, without noise or show, and to pursue your intended route by night. Whether you go by land or water, give out patrol and countersigns in order to recognize one another in the dark, and likewise appoint a station for every man to go to in case of any accident that may separate you.

# APPENDIX E:

# ROGERS' RANGERS STANDING ORDERS

1. Don't forget nothing.
2. Have your musket clean as a whistle, hatchet scoured, sixty rounds powder and ball, and be ready to march at a minute's warning.
3. When you're on the march, act the way you would if you was sneaking up on a deer. See the enemy first.
4. Tell the truth about what you see and what you do. There is an army depending on us for correct information. You can lie all you please when you tell other folks about the Rangers, but don't ever lie to a Ranger or officer.
5. Don't ever take a chance you don't have to.
6. When we're on the march we march single file, far enough apart so one shot can't go through two men.
7. If we strike swamps, or soft ground, we spread out abreast so it's hard to track us.
8. When we march, we keep moving till dark, so as to give the enemy the least possible chance at us.

9.      When we camp, half the party stays awake while the other half sleeps.

10.    If we take prisoners, we keep 'em separate till we have had time to examine them, so they can't cook up a story between 'em.

11.    Don't ever march home the same way. Take a different route so you won't be ambushed.

12.    No matter whether we travel in big parties or little ones, each party has to keep a scout 20 yards ahead, 20 yards on each flank, and 20 yards in the rear so the main body can't be surprised and wiped out.

13.    Every night you'll be told where to meet if surrounded by superior force.

14.    Don't sit down and eat without posting sentries.

15.    Don't sleep beyond dawn. Dawn's when the French and Indians attack.

16.    Don't cross a river by a regular ford.

17.    If somebody's trailing you, make a circle, come back onto your own tracks, and ambush the folks that aim to ambush you.

18.    Don't stand up when the enemy's coming against you. Kneel down, lie down, hide behind a tree.

19.    Let the enemy come till he's almost close enough to touch. Then let him have it and jump out and finish him up with your hatchet.

# APPENDIX F:

As of July 2000
MEMORANDUM FOR: RECORD
SUBJECT: Ranger School Attendance Policy

1. **PURPOSE:** To provide the Commanding General, USAIC facts on Revised policy for attendance at Ranger Course.
2. **BACKGROUND:** The Chief of Staff of the Army directed in Sep 94 who could attend Ranger school as indicated in MESSAGE, CSA, R201600ZSEP94, SUBJECT: RANGER ATTENDANCE POLICY and additional guidance in MESSAGE, ODCSOPS, R301532ZNOV95, EXCEPTION FOR SOF.
3. **FACTS:**
   a. On 101219Z Apr 97 DAMO-TRO provided the guidance listed below on Ranger Attendance Policy.
   b. This message defines which units, officer career management fields, and military occupation specialties are authorized Ranger training. The function of the U.S. Army Ranger Course is to develop the combat arms related functional skills of officer and enlisted volunteers who are eligible for assignment to units whose primary mission is to engage in the close-combat, direct fire battle. Attendance at Ranger School is linked to those who require the special skills developed at this course. The soldiers most likely required to possess these skills are those assigned to the 75th Ranger Regiment; selected Infantrymen in other than Ranger units at the Infantry Battalion and Company level; Special Forces personnel at the A-Team level; Cavalry soldiers at the troop level; Combat Engineers who directly support infantry battalions at the company level; Fire Support personnel habitually associated in direct support to Infantry battalions and air defense personnel habitually associated in direct support

to Infantry battalions. Ranger training is required and/or functionally appropriate for those individuals listed below:

# ELIGIBILITY

(1) **ENLISTED PERSONNEL:** Ranger training is available on a voluntary basis for enlisted soldiers who are in the following MOS:

| | |
|---|---|
| **11B | INFANTRYMAN |
| **11C | INDIRECT FIRE INFANTRYMAN |
| **11 | H HEAVY ANTI-ARMOR WEAPONS INFANTRYMAN |
| **11M | FIGHTING VEHICLE INFANTRYMAN |
| **12B | COMBAT ENGINEER (IN COMPANIES THAT DIRECTLY SUPPORT INFANTRY BATTALIONS) |
| **13F | FIRE SUPPORT SERGEANT (HABITUALLY ASSOCIATED IN DIRECT SUPPORT TO INFANTRY BATTALIONS) |
| **14S | AIR DEFENSE SERGEANTS (HABITUALLY ASSOCIATED IN DIRECT SUPPORT TO INFANTRY BATTALIONS) |
| **CMF 18 | SPECIAL FORCES PERSONNEL |
| **19C | CAVALRY SCOUT |
| **19K | ARMOR CREWMAN |
| ** | THOSE ENLISTED SOLDIERS OF ANY MOS OR SPECIALTY ASSIGNED TO RANGER CODED POSITIONS WITHIN THE 75TH RANGER REGIMENT OR RANGER TRAINING BRIGADE MUST ATTEND. |

(2) **COMMISSIONED OFFICER PERSONNEL:** Ranger training is available for officers in the following career management fields:

| | |
|---|---|
| **11A | INFANTRY OFFICER |
| **12A | ARMOR OFFICER ALLOCATED AGAINST AUTHORIZED 12C POSITIONS |
| **13A | BATTALION AND COMPANY FIRE SUPPORT OFFICERS HABITUALLY ASSOCIATED IN DIRECT SUPPORT TO INFANTRY BATTALIONS |
| **14A | ADA OFFICERS HABITUALLY ASSOCIATED IN DIRECT SUPPORT TO INFANTRY BATTALIONS |
| **18A | SPECIAL FORCES OFFICERS |
| **21B | COMBAT ENGINEER OFFICERS IN COMPANIES THAT DIRECTLY SUPPORT INFANTRY BATTALIONS |
| ** | THOSE OFFICERS OF ANY BRANCH OR SPECIALTY ASSIGNED TO RANGER CODED POSITIONS WITHIN THE 75TH RANGER REGIMENT OR THE RANGER TRAINING BRIGADE MUST ATTEND. |

(3) **UNITS AND SCHOOLS:** Ranger coded positions are limited to the following:

| | |
|---|---|
| ** | SELECTED RANGER REGIMENT POSITIONS |
| ** | SELECTED POSITIONS IN INFANTRY BATTALIONS, COMPANIES, PLATOONS AND LONG-RANGE SURVEILLANCE UNITS |
| ** | SELECTED INSTRUCTORS AT THE INFANTRY SCHOOL |
| ** | SELECTED OBSERVER CONTROLLERS AT THE COMBAT TRAINING CENTERS |
| ** | SELECTED INSTRUCTOR POSITIONS AT THE SCHOOL OF THE AMERICAS |

** SELECTED POSITIONS IN CAVALRY SCOUT TROOPS THAT ARE ASSIGNED TO INFANTRY/ARMOR BATTALIONS AND ARMORED CAVALRY REGIMENTS

** SELECTED POSITIONS IN SPECIAL FORCES A-TEAMS

** SELECTED POSITIONS IN FIRE SUPPORT TEAMS HABITUALLY ASSOCIATED IN DIRECT SUPPORT TO INFANTRY BATTALIONS

** SELECTED POSITIONS IN ENGINEER COMPANIES THAT DIRECTLY SUPPORT INFANTRY BATTALIONS

** SELECTED POSITIONS IN AIR DEFENSE BATTERIES HABITUALLY ASSOCIATED IN DIRECT SUPPORT TO INFANTRY BATTALIONS

c. THIS MESSAGE SUPERSEDES PREVIOUS GUIDANCE (REF 1A AND 1B)

**4. POC**: SENIOR TAC NCIOC, Ranger Training Brigade

# APPENDIX G:

# *RANGER TRAINING*
# *REFERENCES*

It is important that Ranger students arrive to the course as prepared and knowledgeable as possible. Reviewing and studying these references will prove to be of great assistance. While the list is not all-inclusive, it is adequate to plan and conduct Ranger training. During in-processing, students will be issued a "Ranger Handbook". It will serve as your bible.

| REFERENCE | TITLE |
|-----------|-------|
| FM 5-20 | Camouflage, Basic Principles |
| FM 5-25 | Explosives and Demolitions |
| FM 7-10 | The Rifle Squad, Platoon & Company |
| FM 21-11 | First Aid for Soldiers |
| FM 21-20 | Physical Readiness Training |
| FM 21-26 | Map Reading |
| FM 21-50 | Ranger Training |
| FM 21-74 | Patrolling |
| FM 21-75 | Combat Training of the Individual Soldier |
| FM 21-76 | Survival |

| | |
|---|---|
| FM 21-150 | Combatives |
| FM 22-100 | Command and Leadership for the Small Unit Leader |
| FM 22-101 | Counseling |
| FM 30-5 | Combat Intelligence |
| FM 30-101 | The Maneuver Enemy |
| FM 31-21 | Guerrilla Warfare and Special Forces Operations |
| FM 31-72 | Mountain Training |
| FM 72-20 | Jungle Operations |
| TC 7-1 | The Rifle Squad Handbook |
| TC 7-3 | The Rifle Platoon |
| TC 21-1 | Recondo Training |
| TC 22 | Ground Assistance to Helicopter Operations |
| TC 90-61 | Military Mountaineering |
| TC 621-1 | Evasion and Escape Training |
| TM 9-1005-224-10 | Operator Manual, M60 Machine gun |
| TM 9-1010-221-10 | Operator Manual, 40mm Grenade Launcher M203 |
| TM 11-5850-228-13 | Night Vision Sight, Tripod Mounted TM 11- |
| 5855-202-13 | Night Vision Sight, Crew Served Weapons |
| TM 11-5855-203-13 | Night Vision Sight, Individual Weapons |
| ST 7-163 | Artillery Handbook |
| MR 3 | USAIS Communications Handbook |

# APPENDIX H:

# *THE DEFINITION OF*

## *"HOO AAH"*

(*who-a*) adj. [Slang used by soldiers, primarily airborne/RANGERS] referring to or meaning anything and everything except "NO."

1. what to say when at a loss for words.
2. good copy, solid copy, roger, good, great, message received, understood.
3. glad to meet you, welcome.
4. I don't know the answer but I'll check on it, I haven't the vaguest idea.

5. I am not listening.
6. that's enough of your dribble—sit down.
7. stop sniveling.
8. oh shit! you've got to be kidding.
9. yes.
10. thank you.
11. go to the next slide.
12. you've taken the correct action.
13. I don't know what that means, but I'm too embarrassed to ask for clarification.
14. Amen.

**Trivia:** It is believed the origins of this term (one of many cited) evolved with the Second Dragoons in 1841 during a meeting arranged with Chief Coacoochee of the Florida Seminole Indians. Following the meeting, a banquet was held and several toasts, such as 'Here's to luck,' were offered by the Dragoon officers. Explained the meaning of the toasts, Coacoochee raised a cup in return, responding in a deafening, exhilarated voice, "Hough!"

# ENDORSEMENTS FOR
# *TO FIGHT WITH INTREPIDITY...*

Foreword: Only a proud American Army Ranger could have authored such a superb book. Only a proud American Army Ranger could clearly capture in writing the brotherly love, pride, discipline, respect for and loyalty to one another, and belief in the vital importance of mission accomplishment that pervades all U.S. Army Ranger units.

Harold G. Moore
LTG (Ret.)
Co-author
**We Were Soldiers Once ... And Young**

This work of Major John Lock puts the reader on the front lines with some of the most courageous, men in history—the U.S. Army Rangers. To Fight With Intrepidity... provides a compelling look at a very vital combat force.

**Senator Bob Dole**

Major John Lock has provided an exceptional history of our nation's Army Rangers. It is a work and tribute long overdue. I recommend it for anyone interested in our nation's military history.

**Senator J. Robert Kerrey**
**Medal of Honor Recipient**

A fine tribute to a great outfit. From the Revolution to the present, the U.S. Army Rangers have been at the cutting edge. Lock tells the story with skill and passion.

**Stephen E. Ambrose**
**Pulitzer Prize Historian**

Major John Lock's *To Fight With Intrepidity...* is a great achievement. For the first time, the history of the world's premier light infantry force has been written. His scholarly researched description of Rangers in combat through the centuries establishes the rationale for the vigorous training that aspirants for the coveted Ranger-Tab and Ranger Scroll

240

endure. This tough, realistic training and the great demands that Rangers place on themselves are the reasons "Rangers Lead the Way!"

COL (Ret.) Ralph Puckett, Jr.
Honorary Colonel
75th Ranger Regiment

The history of American Rangers is the history of America. When Americans go to war, Rangers lead the way. Now one of their own has taken time to tell their stirring story. And what a story it is! Ranger School graduate John D. Lock writes with an authority and attention to detail certain to make this the definitive history of America's oldest military elite.

Dan Bolger
Author Savage Peace

# Biography: JD Lock

John Lock is a 1982 graduate and former Assistant Professor of the United States Military Academy at West Point who retired from active duty as a Lieutenant Colonel in May 2002. He enlisted in the Army as a private in 1974 and served as a Non-Commissioned Officer until 1978. His commissioned assignments included the 1st Armored Division, West Germany, the 82d Airborne Division, Fort Bragg, N.C., Deputy Commander New York District U.S. Army Corps of Engineers and Deputy/Acting Chief Engineer Stabilization Forces (SFOR), Sarajevo, Bosnia-Herzegovina.

His military and civilian education includes the Engineer Officer Basic Course, the Infantry Officer Advanced Course, the Combined Arms Services Staff School, the Command and General Staff College, and a Master of Science from Rensselaer Polytechnic Institute (RPI). His decorations include the Ranger Tab, Master Parachutists Wings, and the Legion of Merit.

He is the author of *To Fight With Intrepidity: The Complete History of the U.S. Army Rangers, 1622 to Present* (1st edition), published by Simon & Schuster/Pocket Books, 1998 and republished by Fenestra Books (2nd edition), 2001, and the soon to be published *A Legacy of Valor: The Heroic Exploits of the United States Army Rangers.*

In addition to ongoing writing projects—including novels and screenplays, Lock also works in support of architectural development and modeling and simulation for Current Force and the Army's transformation to the Future Force. His Web site is: *http://johndlock.com/* He can be contacted at *JDLock82@aol.com*

Breinigsville, PA USA
10 November 2010
249079BV00001B/238/A

9 781587 363672